FOR THE SUMMER BETWEEN GRADES

4-5

McGraw Hill Children's Publishing
Columbus, Ohio

Copyright © 2003 McGraw-Hill Children's Publishing. Published by American Education Publishing, an imprint of McGraw-Hill Children's Publishing, a Division of The McGraw-Hill Companies.

Printed in the United States of America. All rights reserved. Except as permitted under the United States Copyright Act, no part of this publication may be reproduced or distributed in any form or by any means, or stored in a database or retrieval system, without prior written permission from the publisher, unless otherwise indicated.

Send all inquiries to:
McGraw-Hill Children's Publishing
8787 Orion Place
Columbus, OH 43240-4027

ISBN 1-57768-534-2

1 2 3 4 5 6 7 8 9 10 CJK 08 07 06 05 04 03

Table of Contents

Summer Success Recommended Reading 4
Number Sense 5-9
Number Operations 10-22
Fractions and Decimals 23-25
Measurement 26-32
Geometry 33-40
Logical Thinking 41-44
Vocabulary Strategies 45-47
Language Conventions 48-53
Parts of Speech 54-67
Reading Strategies 68-77
Writing Strategies 78-81
Using Reference Material 82-83
Glossary 84-85
Answer Key 86-94
Skills Checklist 95-96

Recommended Summer Reading Grades 4-5

Autumn Street; Number the Stars; Rabble Starkey	Lois Lowry
Because of Winn-Dixie	Kate Dicamillo
The Birchbark House	Louise Erdrich
Black Beauty	Anna Sewell
Bridge to Terabithia	Katherine Paterson
Bud, Not Buddy	Christopher Paul Curtis
Bunnicula	Deborah Howe
Catherine, Called Birdy	Karen Cushman
Chocolate Covered Ants	Stephen Mares
Crash	Jerry Spinelli
The Cricket in Times Square	George Selden
Dear Mr. Henshaw; Henry and Beezus	Beverly Cleary
Eleanor Roosevelt; A Life of Discovery	Russell Freedman
Encyclopedia Brown Sets the Pace	Donald J. Sobol
Fly Away Home	Eve Bunting
Frindle	Andrew Clements
Harry Potter and the Sorcerer's Stone	J.K. Rowling
Helen Keller's Teacher; Five True Dog Stories	Margaret Davidson
The Indian in the Cupboard; Return of the Indian	Lynne Reid Banks
Insectlopedia	Douglas Florian
Little House on the Prairie	Laura Ingalls Wilder
The Magic School Bus Series	Joanna Cole
Matilda	Roald Dahl
Old Yeller	Fred Gipson
Redwall	Brian Jacques
The Relatives Game	Cynthia Rylant
Sounder	William Howard Armstrong
A Time to Talk: Poems of Friendship	Myra Cohn Livingston
The Truth About Great White Sharks	Mary M. Cerullo
Tuesday	David Wiesner
The Twentieth Century Children's Poetry Treasury	Jack Prelutsky
The Wayside School Series	Louis Sachar
The Wind in the Willows	Kenneth Grahame

Set Sail

Place value is the value of a digit, or numeral, shown by where it is in the number. For example, in 1,234, 1 has the place value of thousands, 2 is hundreds, 3 is tens, and 4 is ones.

Directions: Write the numbers in the correct boxes to find how far the ship has traveled.

one thousand

six hundreds

eight ones

nine ten thousands

four tens

two millions

five hundred thousands

milions	hundred thousands	ten thousands	thousands	hundreds	tens	ones

How many miles has the ship traveled? _____

Directions: In the number . . .

2,386 _____ is in the ones place.

4,957 _____ is in the hundreds place.

102,432 _____ is in the ten thousands place.

489,753 _____ is in the thousands place.

1,743,998 _____ is in the millions place.

9,301,671 _____ is in the hundred thousands place.

7,521,834 _____ is in the tens place.

Name _____

Rounding and Estimating

Rounding numbers and **estimating** answers is an easy way of finding the approximate answer without writing out the problem or using a calculator.

Directions: Fill in the bubble next to the correct answer.

Round to the nearest **ten**:

1. 73 → ○ 70 ○ 80
2. 48 → ○ 40 ○ 50
3. 65 → ○ 60 ○ 70
4. 85 → ○ 80 ○ 90
5. 92 → ○ 90 ○ 100
6. 37 → ○ 30 ○ 40

Round to the nearest **hundred**:

7. 139 → ○ 100 ○ 200
8. 782 → ○ 700 ○ 800
9. 390 → ○ 300 ○ 400
10. 640 → ○ 600 ○ 700
11. 525 → ○ 500 ○ 600
12. 457 → ○ 400 ○ 500

Round to the nearest **thousand**:

13. 1,375 → ○ 1,000 ○ 2,000
14. 21,800 → ○ 21,000 ○ 22,000

15. Sam wanted to buy a new computer. He knew he only had about $1,200 to spend. Which of the following ones could he afford to buy?

 ○ $1,165
 ○ $1,279
 ○ $1,249

16. If Sam spent $39 on software for his new computer, $265 for a printer and $38 for a cordless mouse, about how much money did he need?

_____

6

What Do You Think?

Estimate the answer to each question. Use a timer, watch, or clock that measures seconds to time the activity. Then, record the actual answer. How close was the estimate?

Question	Estimate	Actual Number
1. How many jumping jacks can you do in 15 seconds?		
2. How many seconds does it take to say the alphabet backwards?		
3. How many light bulbs are there in your home?		
4. How many seconds does it take to tie both shoes?		
5. How many times does the letter "p" appear on this page?		
6. How many spoonfuls of water does it take to fill a small drinking glass?		
7. How high can you count aloud in 15 seconds?		
8. How many steps does it take to walk around the edge of the largest room in your home?		
9. How many numbers between 1 and 99 have the numeral 2 in them?		
10. How many seconds does it take to sing "Happy Birthday to You"?		

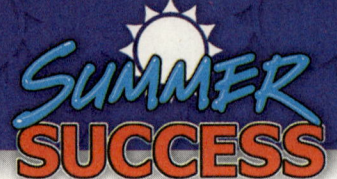

Name _____

Field Day

The winners of the 800-meter relay want to know their winning times. Help them fill in their scores. First, find the mean, mode, and median for each list of numbers. Then, follow the directions below. Remember, the **mean** is the average of the numbers, the **median** is the middle number when the group is put in order, and the **mode** is the number that appears most frequently.

	mean	median	mode
24, 20, 21, 29, 24, 26	_____	_____	_____
24, 26, 22, 26, 28, 30	_____	_____	_____
23, 26, 19, 27, 27, 28, 18	_____	_____	_____

The winning team had a time in seconds equal to the mean of the first problem. The second-place team had a time equal to the median of the second problem. The third-place team had a time equal to the mode of the third problem. Write the times on the cards.

Quacky Comparisons

Circle the box with the sign which should be used when comparing the pair of numbers. Write the letter from the circled box on the matching numbered lines below to answer the riddle.

#	Left	< box	> box	Right
1.	164,982	N <	> F	164,892
2.	27,493,171	C <	> A	27,493,717
3.	13,562,439	R <	> S	13,562,349
4.	60,871,956	M <	> T	60,871,695
5.	34,742	C <	> A	34,472
6.	19,584,578	D <	> K	19,584,785
7.	746,361,294	N <	> L	746,361,492
8.	600,100,001	B <	> Y	600,010,001
9.	88,914,676	N <	> T	88,914,767
10.	41,200,050	Y <	> O	41,200,500
11.	841,762,145	D <	> R	841,762,514
12.	27,181,426	N <	> I	27,181,246
13.	38,226,943	P <	> K	38,226,349
14.	80,000,001	O <	> I	80,000,010
15.	500,146,271	S <	> U	500,146,172
16.	15,836,504	N <	> F	15,836,054
17.	20,673,746	R <	> I	20,673,476

What do ducks call word meanings in their dictionaries?

__ __ __ __ __   __ __ __ __ __ __ __ __ __ __ __
6 15 2 13 8   11 5 16 1 10 7 12 4 17 14 9 3

9

Deep Blue Sea

An **integer** is any positive or negative whole number, or zero. Negative integers are numbers less than zero. The opposite of any number is found the same distance from 0 on a number line.

Example:

$-5\ -4\ -3\ -2\ -1\ 0\ 1\ 2\ 3\ 4\ 5$

35 below zero can be written as -35.
The opposite of 6 is -6.
The opposite of -41 is 41.
The opposite of 0 is 0.

Write a number for each description.
1. 5 feet below sea level _____
2. 14 degrees below zero _____
3. a loss of $10 _____
4. climbing down 9 feet into a cave _____
5. a 2 yard gain in a football game _____
6. 3 fewer fish than the day before _____
7. no change _____
8. driving a car 11 feet in reverse _____

Write a description for each integer.

-6 _____ -14 _____
-3 _____ -7 _____
0 _____ 8 _____
4 _____ -4 _____

Write the opposite number.

6 _____ 0 _____
4 _____ -14 _____
-9 _____ -7 _____
5 _____ 25 _____

10

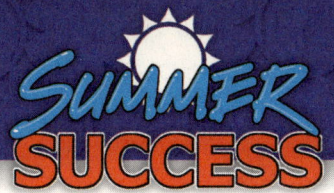

Pattern Puzzles

Figuring out the secret to a number pattern or code can send you into "thinking overtime."

Directions: Discover the pattern for each set of numbers. Then write the missing numbers.

a) 20, 21, 19, 20, 18, 19, 17, _____, 16, 17, 15, _____, _____, _____, _____, _____.

b) 1, 6, 16, 31, 51, _____, _____, 141, _____, 226.

c) 3, 5, 9, 15, _____, _____, 45, _____, 75.

d) 55, 52, 50, 49, 46, _____, _____, _____, _____, _____, 34.

e) 1, 3, 6, 10, 15, 21, _____, _____, _____, 55, 66, 78.

f) 10, 16, 13, 19, 16, _____, 19, _____, _____, 28, _____.

g) 3, 4, 7, 12, _____, _____, 39, _____, 67, _____.

h) 100, 90, 95, 85, 90, 80, 85, _____, _____, _____, 75.

Directions: Make up a number pattern of your own. Have a parent, brother or sister figure it out!

_____, _____, _____, _____, _____, _____, _____, _____, _____, _____.

Directions: Follow the instructions to solve the number puzzler.

Use only these numbers: 2, 4, 5, 7, 8, 11, 13, 14, 16.

Each number may only be used once.

Write even numbers in the squares.

Write odd numbers in the circles.

Each row must add up to 26.

Hint: Work the puzzle in pencil, so you can erase and retry numbers if needed.

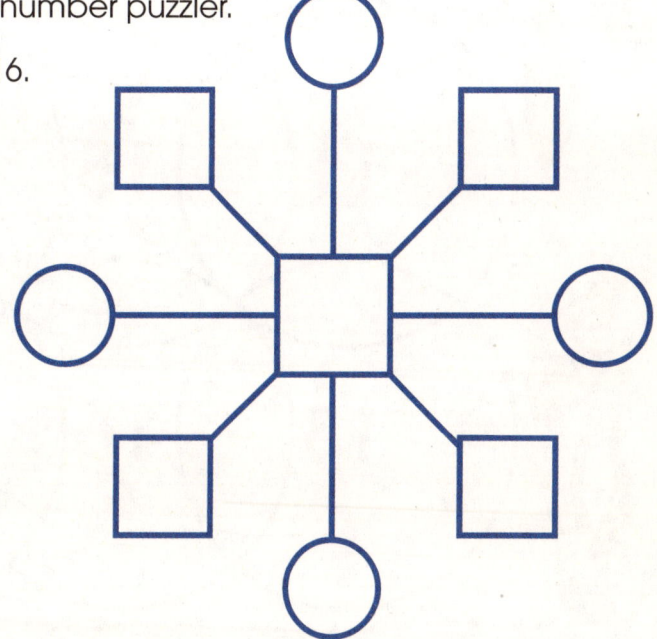

11

Going in Circles

Directions: Where the circles meet, write the sum of the numbers from the circles on the right and left and above and below. The first row shows you what to do.

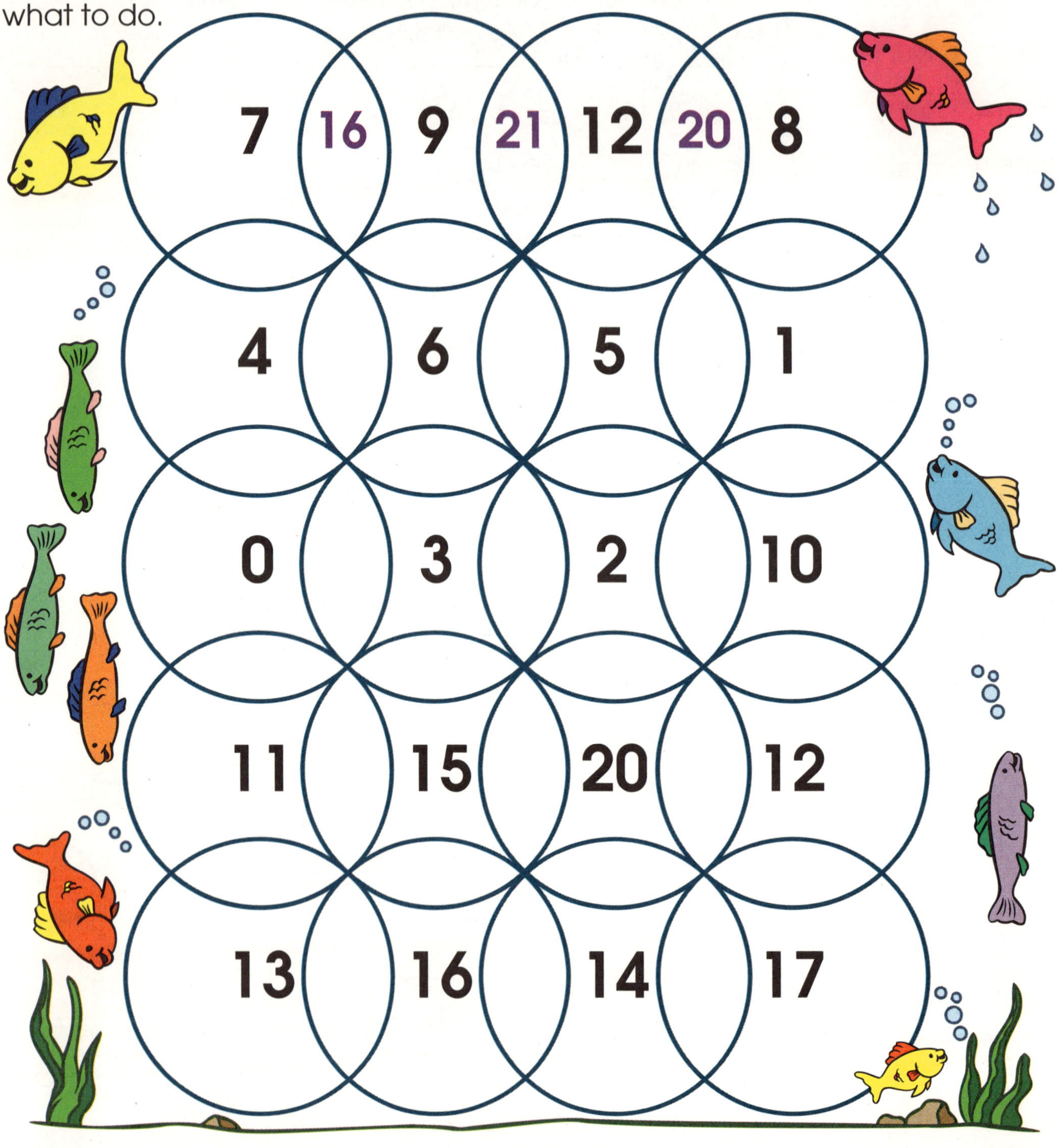

7   16   9   21   12   20   8

4   6   5   1

0   3   2   10

11   15   20   12

13   16   14   17

12

Bringing Fido Home

Regrouping uses 10 ones to form one 10, 10 tens to form one hundred, one 10 and 5 ones to form 15, and so on.

Directions: Add using regrouping. Color in all the boxes with a 5 in the answer to help the dog find its way home.

	63 + 22	5,268 4,910 + 1,683	248 + 463	291 + 543	2,934 + 112
1,736 + 5,367	2,946 + 7,384	3,245 1,239 + 981	738 + 692	896 + 728	594 + 738
2,603 + 5,004	4,507 + 289	1,483 + 6,753	1,258 + 6,301	27 469 + 6,002	4,637 + 7,531
782 + 65	485 + 276	3,421 + 8,064			
48 93 + 26	90 263 + 864	362 453 + 800			

13

Name _____

Snack Subtract

Directions: Subtract using regrouping.

Examples:

```
    23       ¹1
           2̷ ³3
  - 18     - 18
           ────
              5
```

```
   243      ¹ ¹³
          2̷ 4̷ ³3
  - 96     - 9 6
           ──────
           1 4 7
```

81 - 53	76 - 49	94 - 38	156 - 77	341 - 83	726 - 29
568 - 173	806 - 738	743 - 550	903 - 336	647 - 289	254 - 69
730 - 518	961 - 846	573 - 76	604 - 55	265 - 19	372 - 59
111 - 82	358 - 99	147 - 49			
180 - 106	325 - 68	873 - 35			

14

Name _____

Stocking Sue's Pond

Directions: Add or subtract, using regrouping when needed.

```
   38        1,269                      629
   43        2,453      5,792           491       4,697
 + 21      + 8,219    - 4,814         + 308     - 2,988
 ____      _____    _____         _____     _____


               68        197
  5,280        27        436         7,321        456
- 3,147      + 42      + 213       - 2,789      + 974
_____      ____      _____       _____      _____


              492
  3,932       863      9,873        4,978       6,235
+ 4,681      + 57    + 5,483      + 2,131     + 2,986
_____      ____    _____      _____     _____
```

Sue stocked her pond with 263 bass and 187 trout. 97 fish swam away in a flood. How many fish are left?

_____

Bragging Rights

Directions: Round the numbers to the nearest hundred. Then solve the problems.

Example:
Jack and Alex were playing a computer game. Jack scored 428 points. Alex scored 132. About how many more points did Jack score than Alex?

Round Jack's 428 points down to the nearest hundred, 400.

Round Alex's 132 points down to 100. Subtract.

estimate
$$\begin{array}{r} 400 \\ -100 \\ \hline 300 \end{array}$$

$\begin{array}{r}258 \rightarrow 300 \\ +117 \rightarrow +100 \\ \hline 375 400\end{array}$	$\begin{array}{r}493 \rightarrow \\ +114 \rightarrow \\ \hline \end{array}$	$\begin{array}{r}837 \rightarrow \\ -252 \rightarrow \\ \hline \end{array}$
$\begin{array}{r}928 \rightarrow \\ -437 \rightarrow \\ \hline \end{array}$	$\begin{array}{r}700 \rightarrow \\ -491 \rightarrow \\ \hline \end{array}$	$\begin{array}{r}319 \rightarrow \\ +630 \rightarrow \\ \hline \end{array}$
$\begin{array}{r}332 \rightarrow \\ +567 \rightarrow \\ \hline \end{array}$	$\begin{array}{r}493 \rightarrow \\ -162 \rightarrow \\ \hline \end{array}$	$\begin{array}{r}1{,}356 \rightarrow \\ +2{,}941 \rightarrow \\ \hline \end{array}$

Name _____

Lots of Fish in the Sea

When multiplying a number by 10, the answer is the number with a 0. It is like counting by tens.

Examples:

10	10	10	10	10	10
x 1	x 2	x 3	x 4	x 5	x 6
10	20	30	40	50	60

When multiplying a number by 100, the answer is the number with two 0's. When multiplying by 1,000, the answer is the number with three 0's.

Examples:

100	100	100	1,000	1,000	1,000
x 1	x 2	x 3	x 1	x 2	x 3
100	200	300	1,000	2,000	3,000

4	400	8	800	7	700
x 2	x 2	x 3	x 3	x 5	x 5
8	800	24	2,400	35	3,500

Directions: Multiply.

17

Birds of a Feather

Directions: Multiply.

```
   25        70       844       124
  x72       x66      x 24      x 15
```

```
   45        76        74       261
  x41       x78       x69      x 88
```

```
   48       263        37        52
  x36      x  57       x64      x43
```

```
  321       544       797       998
  x 78      x 58      x 24      x 37
```

```
  249        24        48       817
  x 33      x19       x20       x 59
```

18

A Worm Divided

Division is a way to find out how many times one number is contained in another number. For example, 28 ÷ 7 = 4 means that there are 4 groups of 7 in 28.

Division problems can be written two ways: 36 ÷ 6 = 6 or 6)$\overline{36}$

These are the parts of a division problem: dividend ⟶ 36 ÷ 6 = 6 ⟵ quotient
divisor

divisor ⟶ 6)$\overline{36}$ ⟵ quotient / dividend

Directions: Divide.

1)$\overline{7}$ 2)$\overline{2}$ 5)$\overline{25}$ 4)$\overline{32}$ 2)$\overline{4}$ 3)$\overline{6}$

9)$\overline{45}$

4)$\overline{12}$ 8)$\overline{24}$ 6)$\overline{24}$ 9)$\overline{54}$ 5)$\overline{15}$ 3)$\overline{9}$

7)$\overline{14}$

6)$\overline{12}$

6)$\overline{36}$ 6)$\overline{48}$ 5)$\overline{40}$ 3)$\overline{75}$

81 ÷ 9 = ____   64 ÷ 8 = ____   63 ÷ 7 = ____

72 ÷ 8 = ____

72 ÷ 9 = ____   27 ÷ 3 = ____   16 ÷ 4 = ____

19

Name _____

Farming for Answers

Directions: Divide. Then check each answer on another sheet of paper by multiplying it by the divisor and adding the remainder.

Example:

```
       2
12)256
  -24
    1
```

```
      21 R4
12)256
  -24
    16
   -12
     4
```

Check:

```
     21
  x 12
    42
   210
   252
  +  4
   256
```

27)880   81)913   65)790   42)674   67)823

72)977   54)743   45)863   24)432   18)378

28)175   49)538   77)936   37)603   63)835

The Allen farm has 882 chickens. The chickens are kept in 21 coops. How many chickens are there in each coop? _____

20

Fact Families

A fact family shows how division and multiplication are related.

Example:

Here is the fact family for 4, 8, and 32.

4 x 8 = 32
8 x 4 = 32
32 ÷ 4 = 8
32 ÷ 8 = 4

Write the missing numbers in each fact family.

2 x 6 = 12   8 x 3 = 24   _____ x 9 = 81

_____ x 2 = 12   _____ x 8 = 24   9 x 9 = _____

12 ÷ 6 = _____   24 ÷ 3 = _____   81 ÷ _____ = 9

_____ ÷ 2 = 6   24 ÷ 8 = _____   _____ ÷ 9 = 9

4 x 6 = _____   8 x 2 = _____   10 x _____ = 110

6 x _____ = 24   2 x 8 = _____   11 x _____ = 110

_____ ÷ 6 = 4   16 ÷ _____ = 8   _____ ÷ 11 = 10

24 ÷ 4 = _____   16 ÷ 8 = _____   110 ÷ 10 = _____

21

Name _____

Too Much or Too Little

Word problems may give more information than needed. When solving that kind of problem, ignore the extra information. Some word problems are missing needed information. Sometimes the information in a table, graph, or diagram may help. Other times, you will not be able to solve the problem.

CHICKEN SALAD
serves 4

2 cups chopped chicken
1 cup mayonnaise
1 cup celery
1 cup walnuts

Mix together. Refrigerate for 1 hour.

Example:

1. TOO MUCH INFORMATION
   Carmen has 3 cups of chicken, 2 cups of mayonnaise, and plenty of celery and walnuts. If she makes the recipe, how much chicken is left over? Solution: 1 cup; you do not need to know how much mayo there is.

2. FIND MISSING INFORMATION
   How many cups of walnuts are needed to make enough chicken salad to serve 8 people? Solution: 2 cups; look at the recipe to find serving size in order to solve the problem.

3. NOT ENOUGH INFORMATION
   How many cups of celery does Drew need to feed the people at his party? Solution: you cannot solve this problem; you need to know how many people are coming to the party.

Use the recipe card to solve these problems. If there is not enough information, write what you would need to solve it.

1. If a cook has 3 cups of walnuts and enough of all the other ingredients, how many people can be served? _____

2. Cathy replaces some of the celery with carrots. How much celery is still in the recipe? _____

3. Sarah uses 2 cups of chicken, 1 cup of walnuts, and 1 cup of celery. How many more cups of chicken are there than celery? _____

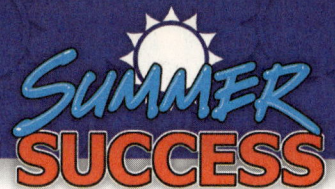

Under the Big Top

Directions: Compare the fraction to the decimal in each box. Circle the larger number.

Example: ($\frac{1}{4}$) 0.1

fourths

tenths

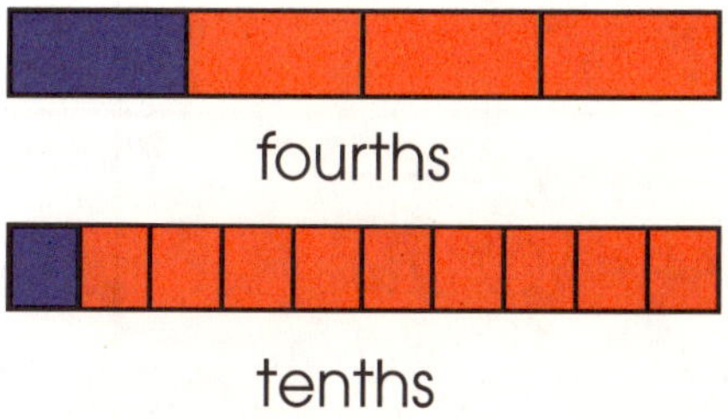

| $\frac{2}{4}$ 0.2 | $\frac{3}{4}$ 0.3 | $\frac{1}{2}$ 0.6 | $\frac{1}{4}$ 0.4 | $\frac{1}{3}$ 0.1 |

| $\frac{1}{4}$ 0.7 | $\frac{2}{4}$ 0.8 | $\frac{3}{4}$ 0.9 | $\frac{5}{6}$ 0.5 | $\frac{2}{5}$ 0.6 |

| $\frac{3}{12}$ 0.9 | $\frac{1}{6}$ 0.2 | $\frac{2}{3}$ 0.8 | $\frac{1}{5}$ 0.3 | $\frac{2}{5}$ 0.7 |

| $\frac{3}{10}$ 0.5 | $\frac{1}{9}$ 0.4 | $\frac{4}{5}$ 0.7 | $\frac{1}{3}$ 0.7 | $\frac{6}{12}$ 0.1 |

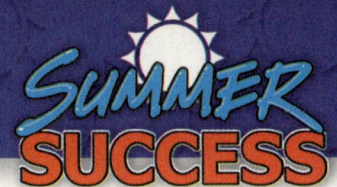

Name _____

Decimal Delivery

Directions: Add or subtract the problems. Then fill in the bubble next to the correct answer.

Example:
2.4
+ 1.7
─────
○ 2.5
○ 3.1
● 4.1

2.8 + 3.4 ○ 5.2 ○ 7.4 ○ 6.2	5.7 − 3.8 ○ 1.9 ○ 2.5 ○ 2.9	7.6 + 8.9 ○ 15.9 ○ 16.5 ○ 17.3
16.3 + 9.8 ○ 25.11 ○ 26.1 ○ 26.01	28.6 +43.9 ○ 73.6 ○ 72.5 ○ 71.9	43.9 + 56.5 ○ 100.4 ○ 107.4 ○ 101.4
12.87 − 3.45 ○ 16.32 ○ 10.31 ○ 9.42	47.56 − 33.95 ○ 13.61 ○ 80.41 ○ 14.61	93.6 − 79.8 ○ 14.8 ○ 15.3 ○ 13.8
11.57 +10.64 ○ 22.21 ○ 1.93 ○ 21.12	27.83 − 14.94 ○ 14.09 ○ 12.89 ○ 11.97	106.935 − 95.824 ○ 111.1 ○ 111.11 ○ 11.111

The high-speed train traveled 87.90 miles on day one, 127.86 miles on day two and 113.41 miles on day three. How many miles did it travel in all? _____

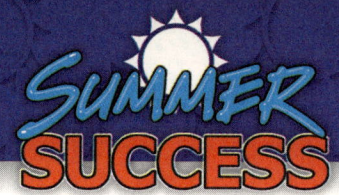

Name _____

At the Science Store

Solve. Remember to align the decimal points.

1. Mr. Fargas buys 2 books. How much does he spend?

   $19.98

   ```
      1 1
   $ 9.99
   +$ 9.99
   $19.98
   ```

Telescope	$75.15
Geode	$13.50
Rock set	$ 5.95
Book	$ 9.99
Chemistry set	$26.59
Fossils small	$ 8.79
large	$12.89
Star chart	$21.47
Pendulum	$18.64

Tax included in prices!

2. Janice buys a star chart and a pendulum. How much does she spend?

   _____

5. Oliver buys *Dinosaurs, The Great Ice Age* and *Rocks of Hawaii*. How much will his books cost?

   _____

3. Can Troy buy a chemistry set and a rock set for less than $30?

   _____

6. Find the price of a large fossil, the chemistry set, and a telescope.

   _____

4. Jack buys a rock set and pendulum. He pays with a $20 bill and a $10 bill. How much change does he receive?

   _____

25

Household Measurements

An **inch** is a unit of length in the standard system equal to $\frac{1}{12}$ of a foot. A ruler is used to measure inches.

This illustration shows a ruler measuring a 4-inch pencil, which can be written as 4" or 4 in.

Directions: Use a ruler to measure each object to the nearest inch.

1. The length of your foot _____
2. The width of your hand _____
3. The length of this page _____
4. The width of this page _____
5. The length of a large paper clip _____
6. The length of your toothbrush _____
7. The length of a comb _____
8. The height of a juice glass _____
9. The length of your shoe _____
10. The length of a fork _____

A Day at the Amusement Park

Directions: Use a ruler to find the shortest paths. Round your measurement to the nearest quarter inch. Then convert to yards using the scale.

Scale: 1 inch = 100 yards

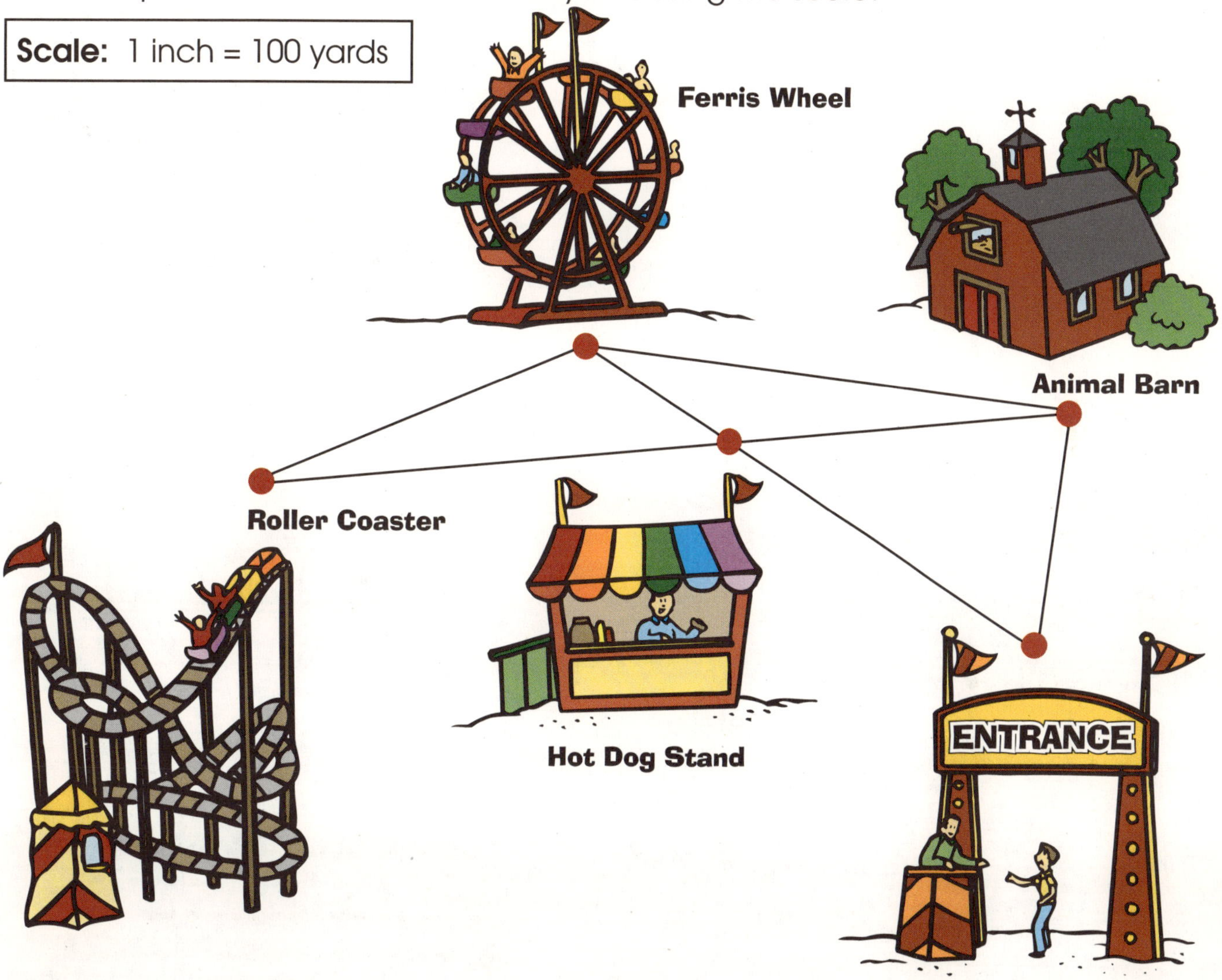

Hot dog stand to the roller coaster . . . _____

The Ferris wheel to the animal barn . . . _____

Entrance to roller coaster . . . _____

Animal barn to hot dog stand . . . _____

Ferris wheel to roller coaster to entrance . . . _____

27

Comparing Measurements

Directions: Use the symbols greater than (>), less than (<) or equal to (=) to complete each statement.

10 inches _____ 10 centimeters

40 feet _____ 120 yards

25 grams _____ 25 kilograms

16 quarts _____ 4 gallons

2 liters _____ 2 milliliters

16 yards _____ 6 meters

3 miles _____ 3 kilometers

20 centimeters _____ 20 meters

85 kilograms _____ 8 grams

2 liters _____ 1 gallon

1 gallon = 3.78 liters
1 meter = 100 centimeters
1 mile = 1.60 kilometers
1 meter = 1.09 yards
1 liter = 1000 milliliters
1 gallon = 4 quarts
1 kilogram = 1000 grams
1 yard = 3 feet
1 inch = 3.54 centimeters

28

Name _____

Temperature

The customary unit of temperature is the degree **Fahrenheit** (°F). A thermometer is used to measure temperature.

Examples:

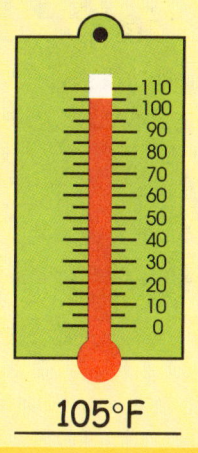
105°F

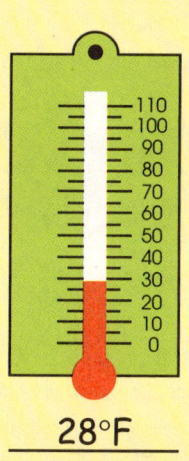
28°F

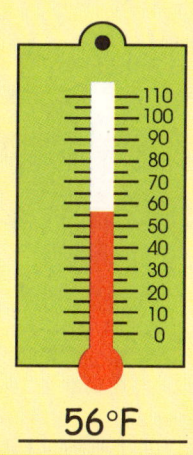
56°F

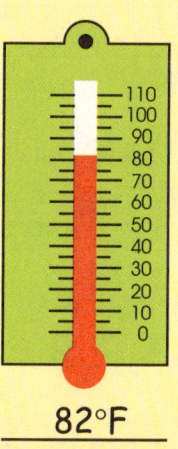
82°F

Write the temperature shown on each thermometer.

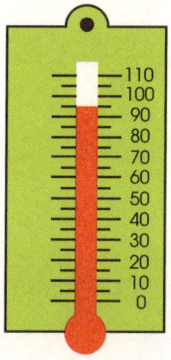

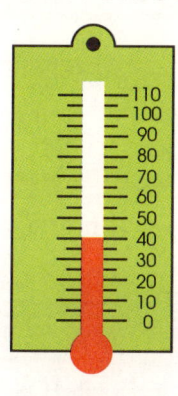

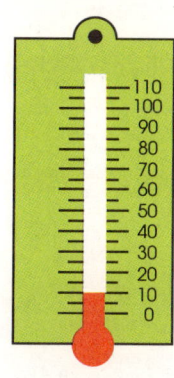

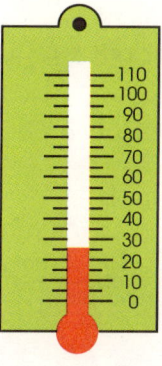

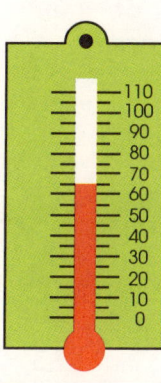

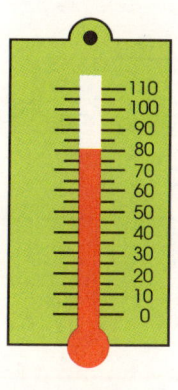

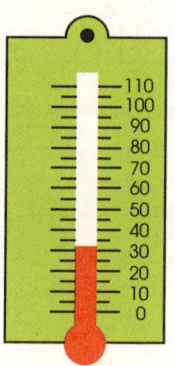

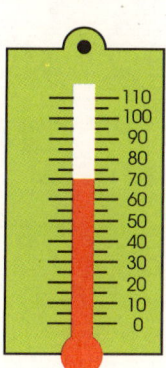

Heavyweights

Weight measures the force of gravity applied to an object. The customary units for weight are the **ounce**, **pound**, and **ton**.

Examples:

A large strawberry weighs about 1 ounce.

A hardcover book weighs about 1 pound.

A small car weighs about 1 ton.

Write **ounce**, **pound**, or **ton** to fill in the blanks in the story.

I enjoy working at Vincent's candy store. Every morning a 12- _____ truck arrives to deliver candy. Very large, 50- _____ boxes filled with chocolates, jelly beans, and lollipops are unloaded in the back room. We divide the candy in each box into 1- _____ decorative boxes to sell to the customers. Many people buy just a few pieces, and we weigh them on a scale. Each piece might weigh 1 or 2 _____. Sometimes, Mr. Vincent lets us take home candy or try new samples at the store. I think I will gain 50 _____ working there!

Write a story that includes the words **ounce**, **pound**, and **ton**.

_____

_____

_____

30

Perimeter and Area

Perimeter is the distance around a figure. It is found by adding the lengths of the sides. **Area** is the number of square units needed to cover a region. The area is found by adding the number of square units. A unit can be any unit of measure. Most often, inches, feet or yards are used.

Directions: Find the perimeter and area for each figure. The first one is done for you.

 = 1 square unit

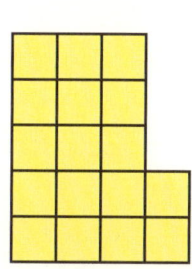
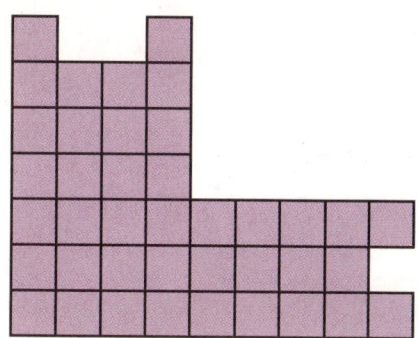

Perimeter = __18__ units   Perimeter = _____ units   Perimeter = _____ units
Area = __17__ sq. units   Area = _____ sq. units   Area = _____ sq. units

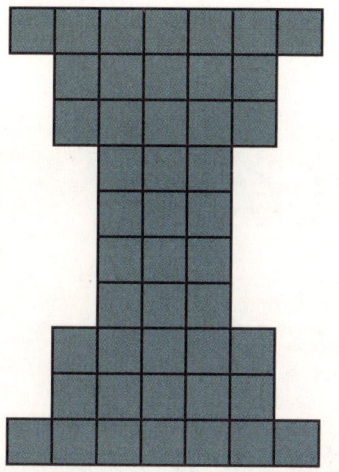
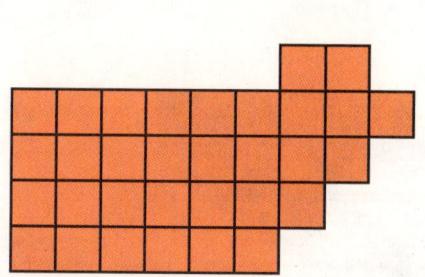

Perimeter = _____ units   Perimeter = _____ units   Perimeter = _____ units
Area = _____ sq. units   Area = _____ sq. units   Area = _____ sq. units

31

Name _____

How Much Does It Hold?

Volume is the measurement of capacity. The formula for finding the volume of a box is length times width times height **(L x W x H)**. The answer is given in cubic units.

Directions: Solve the problems.

Example:

Height 8 ft.
Length 8 ft.
Width 8 ft. **L x W x H = volume**
8' x 8' x 8' = 512 cubic ft. or 512 ft.³

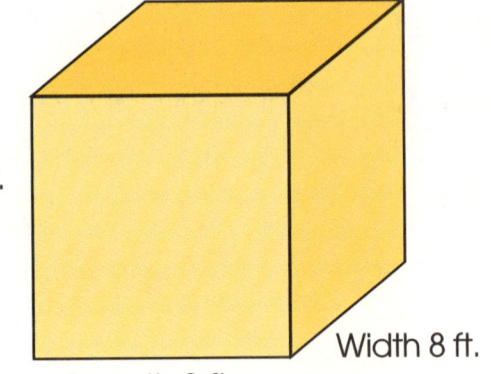

V = _____

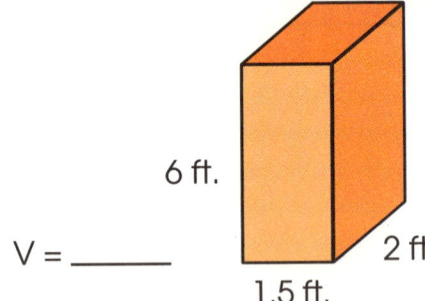

V = _____

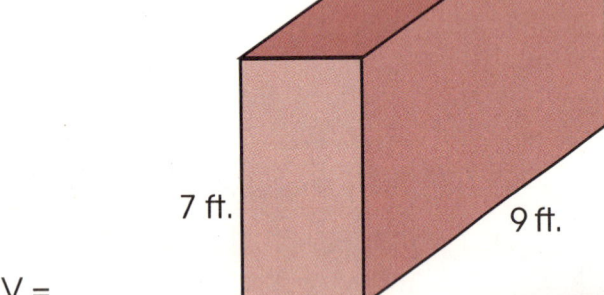

V = _____

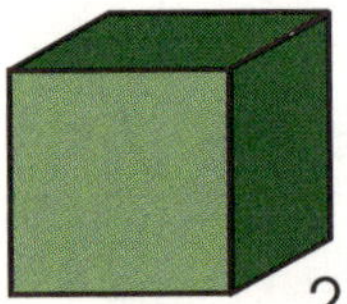

V = _____

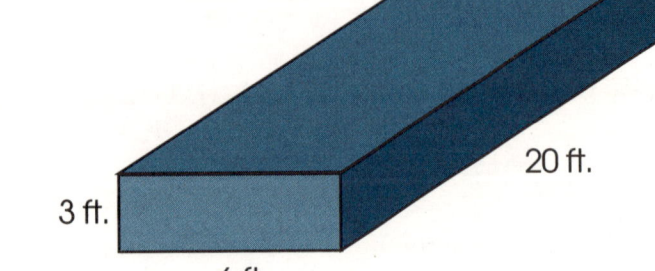

V = _____

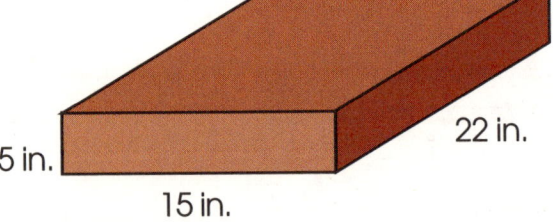

V = _____ in.³   V = _____ ft.³

32

Lines

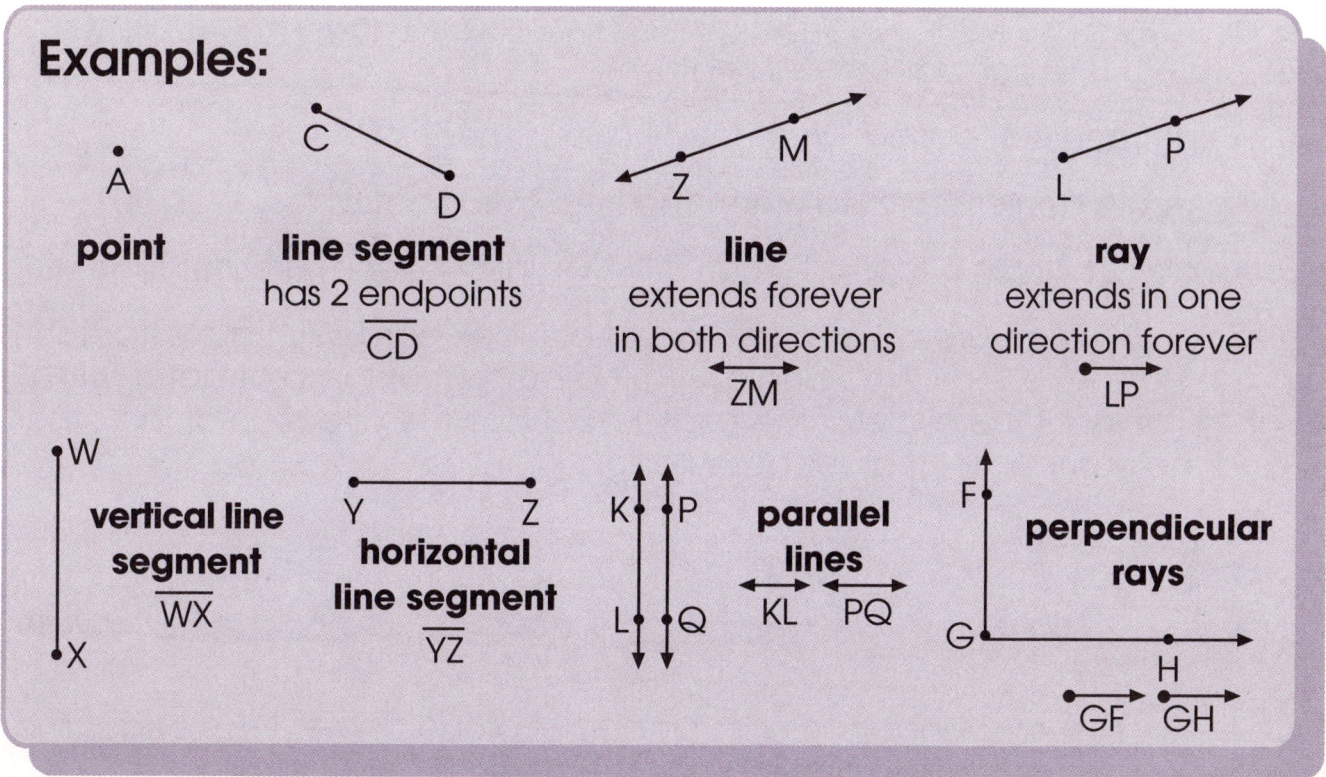

Describe each object using words and symbols.

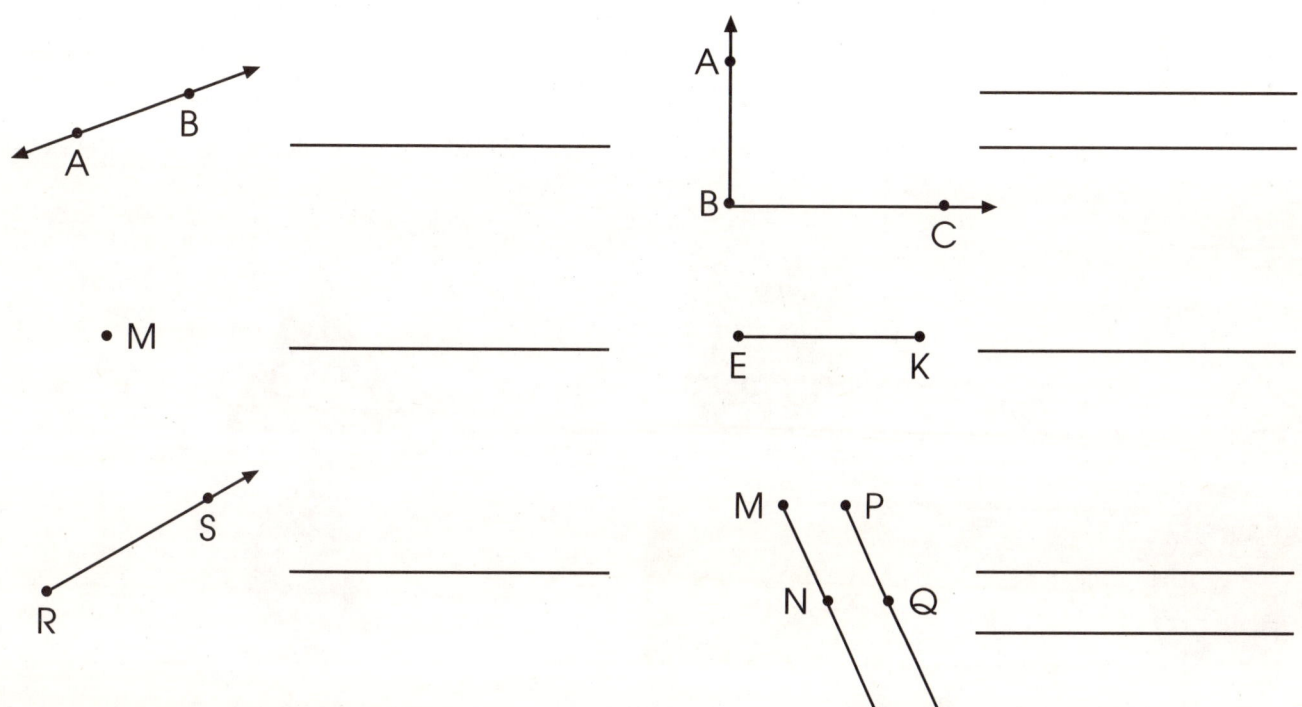

33

Name _____

Angles

The point at which two line segments meet is called an **angle**. There are three types of angles — right, acute and obtuse.

A **right angle** is formed when the two lines meet at 90°.

An **acute angle** is formed when the two lines meet at less than 90°.

An **obtuse angle** is formed when the two lines meet at greater than 90°.

Angles can be measured with a protractor or index card. With a protractor, align the bottom edge of the angle with the bottom of the protractor, with the angle point at the circle of the protractor. Note the direction of the other ray and the number of degrees of the angle.

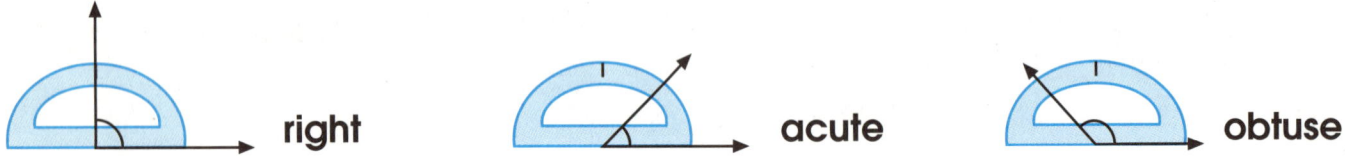

Place the corner of an index card in the corner of the angle. If the edges line up with the card, it is a right angle. If not, the angle is acute or obtuse.

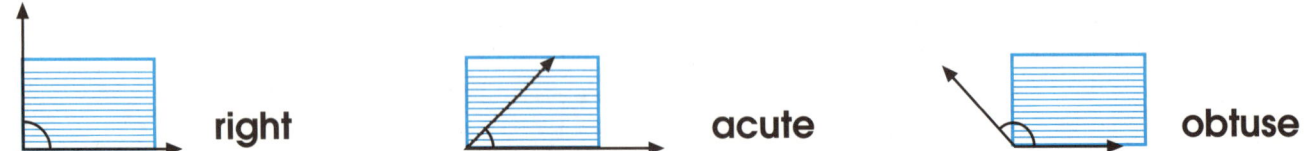

Directions: Use a protractor or index card to identify the following angles as right, obtuse or acute.

34

Name _____

Angles

When two line segments come together, they form an angle.

angle BAC
∠ BAC
∠ A

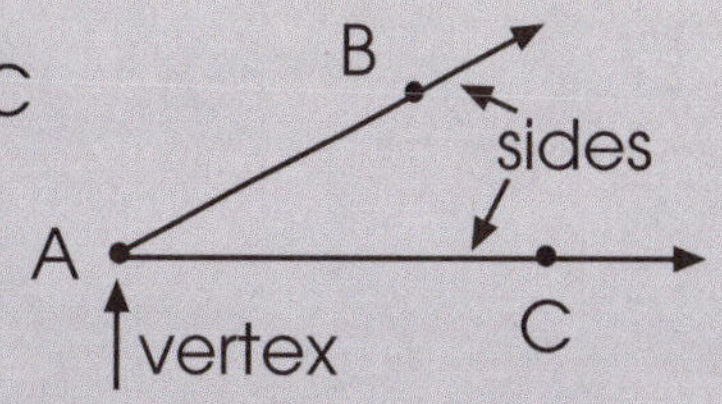

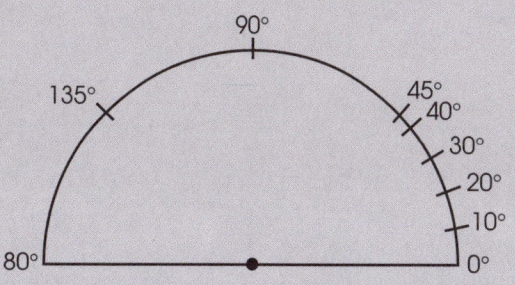

Angles are measured in units called degrees (°). A half-circle has 180°. Angles can be measured with a protractor.

The number of degrees in an angle determines what kind of angle it is.

acute angle
less than 90°

right angle
exactly 90°

obtuse angle
more than 90°

Name each angle and classify it as acute, right, or obtuse.

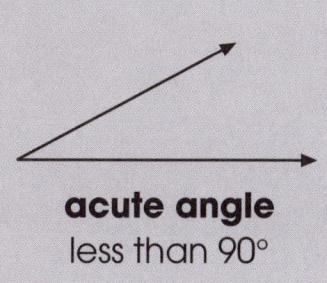

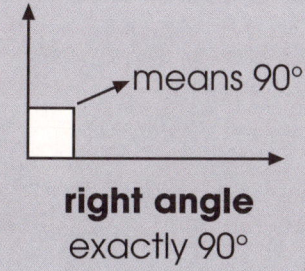

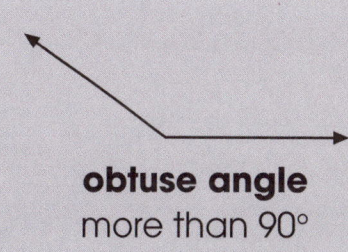

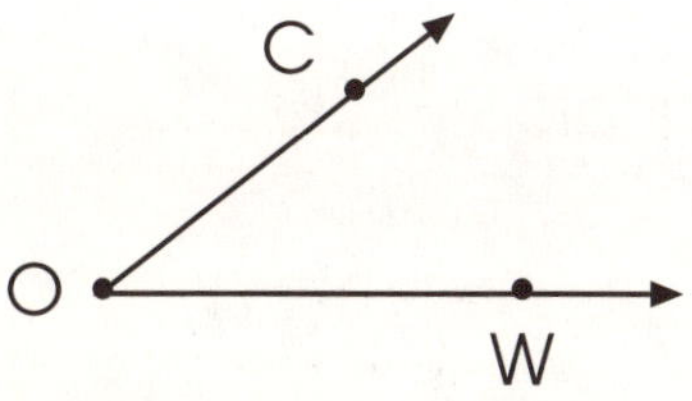

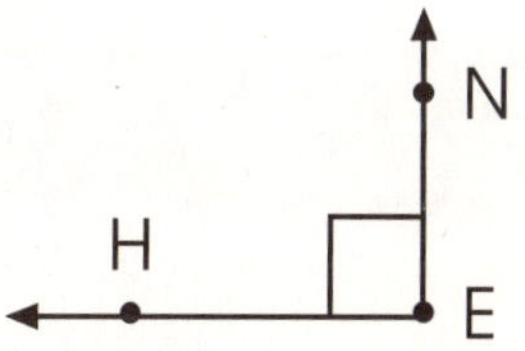

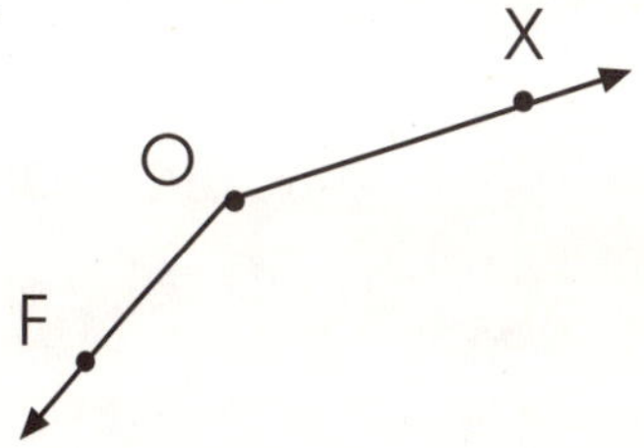

_____   _____   _____

Draw each angle.

acute angle CAT   obtuse angle DOG   right angle PIG

35

Name _____

Triangle Groups

Triangles can also be classified by the kinds of angles they have.

acute
all three angles less than 90°

right
one angle is exactly 90°

obtuse
one angle is more than 90°

An **isosceles** triangle is a triangle with at least two equal sides.

Draw each triangle.

acute triangle

right triangle

obtuse triangle

obtuse isosceles triangle

Name _____

Circles

A **circle** is a round figure. It is named by its center. A **radius** is a line segment from the center of a circle to any point on the circle. A **diameter** is a line segment with both end points on the circle. The diameter always passes through the center of the circle.

Directions: Name the radius, diameter and circle.

Example:

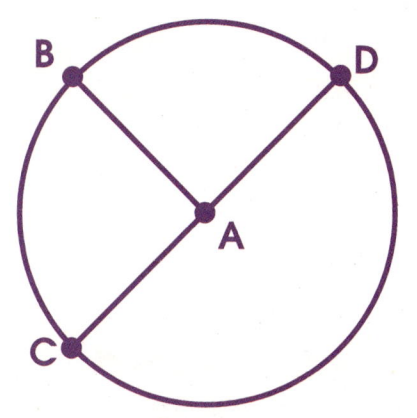

Circle ___A___
Radius ___AB___
Diameter ___DC___

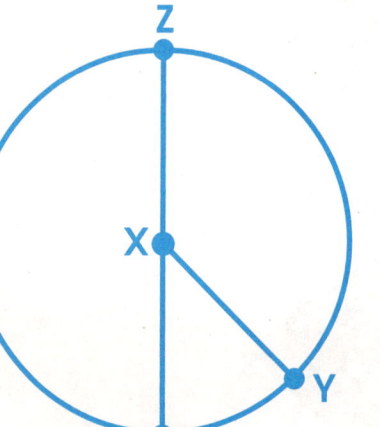

Circle _____
Radius _____
Diameter _____

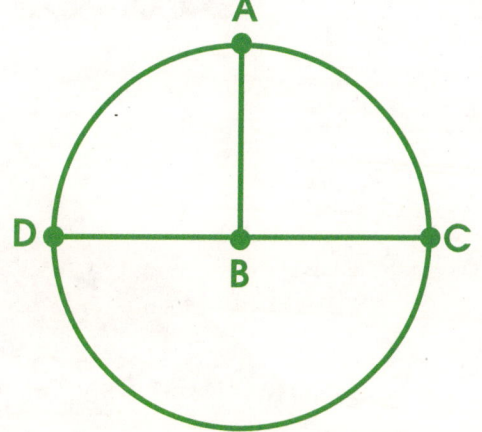

Circle _____
Radius _____
Diameter _____

Name _____

Polygons

A **polygon** is a closed figure with three or more sides.

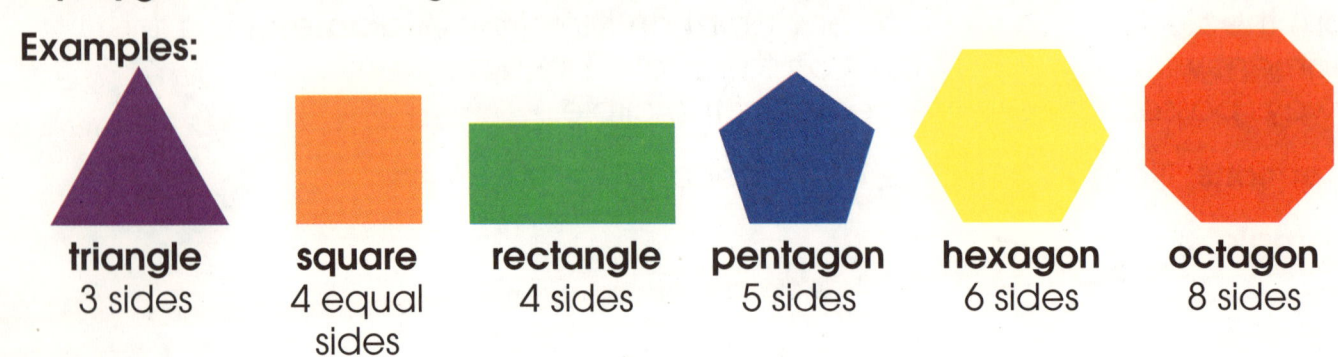

Examples:

triangle	square	rectangle	pentagon	hexagon	octagon
3 sides	4 equal sides	4 sides	5 sides	6 sides	8 sides

Directions: Identify the polygons.

_____

_____

_____

_____

_____

_____

Similar, Congruent, and Symmetrical Figures

Similar figures have the same shape but have varying sizes.

Figures that are **congruent** have identical shapes but different orientations. That means they face in different directions.

Symmetrical figures can be divided equally into two identical parts.

Directions: Cross out the shape that does not belong in each group. Label the two remaining shapes as similiar, congruent or symmetrical.

What's Next?

Draw the next three shapes in the pattern.

Draw a pattern that uses shapes. Have another person draw the next three shapes in the pattern.

_____   _____   _____   _____   _____

_____   _____   _____   _____   _____

40

Graphs

Directions: Read each graph and follow the directions.

List the names of the students from the shortest to the tallest.

1. _____   4. _____
2. _____   5. _____
3. _____   6. _____

Heights of Students (bar graph)
- Andy: 5'0"
- Tiffany: 4'10"
- Louis: 5'1"
- Stephie: 5'6"
- Michele: 4'11"
- Jessie: 5'2"

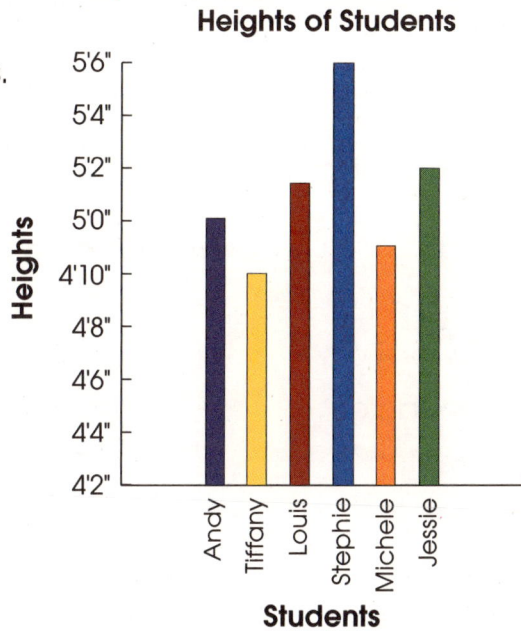

Lunches Bought (line graph)
- Monday: 82
- Tuesday: 73
- Wednesday: 85
- Thursday: 78
- Friday: 92

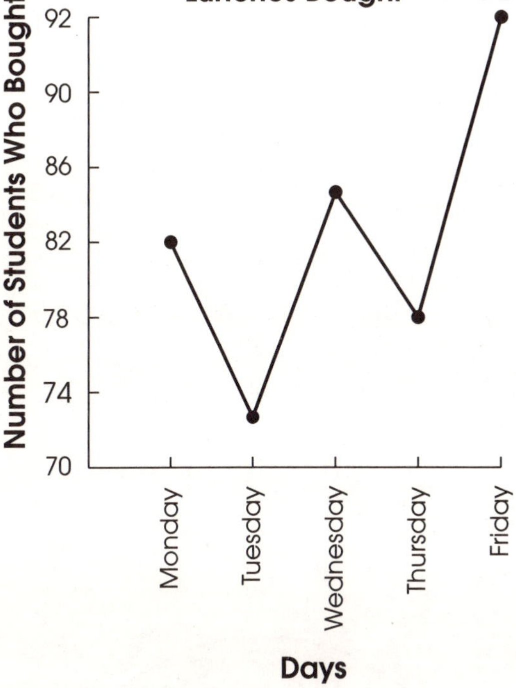

List how many lunches the students bought each day, from the day the most were bought to the least.

1. _____   4. _____
2. _____   5. _____
3. _____

Days of Outside Recess (line graph)
- September: 18
- October: 16
- November: 14
- December: 8
- January: 10
- February: 12
- March: 15
- April: 18
- May: 19
- June: 20

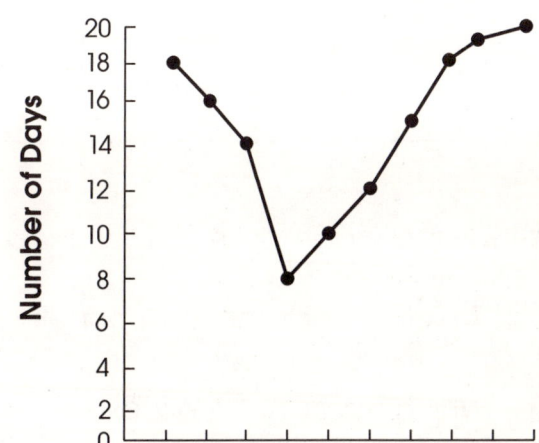

List the months in the order of the most number of outside recesses to the least number.

1. _____   6. _____
2. _____   7. _____
3. _____   8. _____
4. _____   9. _____
5. _____   10. _____

41

Name _____

Graphing Data

Directions: Complete the following exercises.

1. Use the following information to create a bar graph.

Cities	Population (in 1,000's)
Dover	20
Newton Falls	12
Springdale	25
Hampton	17
Riverside	5

2. Study the data and create a line graph showing the number of baskets Jonah scored during the season.

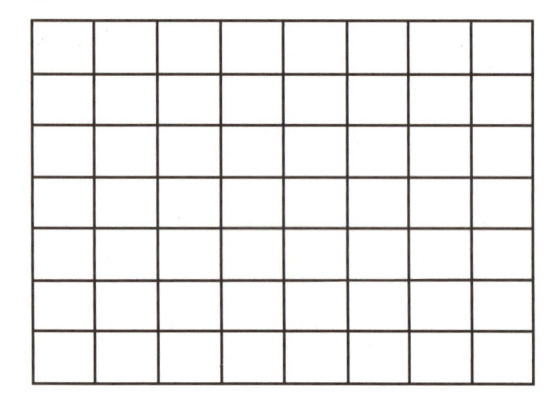

   Game 1 — 10
   Game 2 — 7
   Game 3 — 11
   Game 4 — 10
   Game 5 — 9
   Game 6 — 5
   Game 7 — 9

   Fill in the blanks.
   a. High game: _____
   b. Low game: _____
   c. Average baskets per game: _____

3. Study the graph, then answer the questions.

   a. Which flavor is the most popular? _____

   b. Which flavor sold the least? _____

   c. What decimal represents the two highest sellers? _____

   d. Which flavor had $\frac{1}{10}$ of the sales? _____

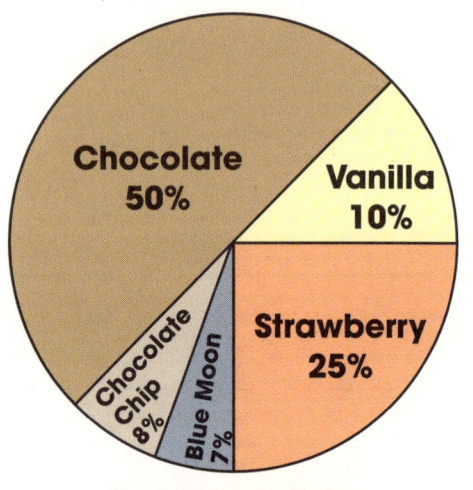

   Ice-Cream Sales
   - Chocolate 50%
   - Vanilla 10%
   - Strawberry 25%
   - Chocolate Chip 8%
   - Blue Moon 7%

42

Name _____

Location, Location, Location

To locate points on a grid, read the first coordinate and follow it to the second coordinate.

Example: C, 3

Directions: Maya is new in town. Help her learn the way around her new neighborhood. Place the following locations on the grid below.

Grocery	C, 10
Home	B, 2
School	A, 12
Playground	B, 13
Library	D, 6
Bank	G, 1
Post Office	E, 7
Ice-Cream Shop	D, 3

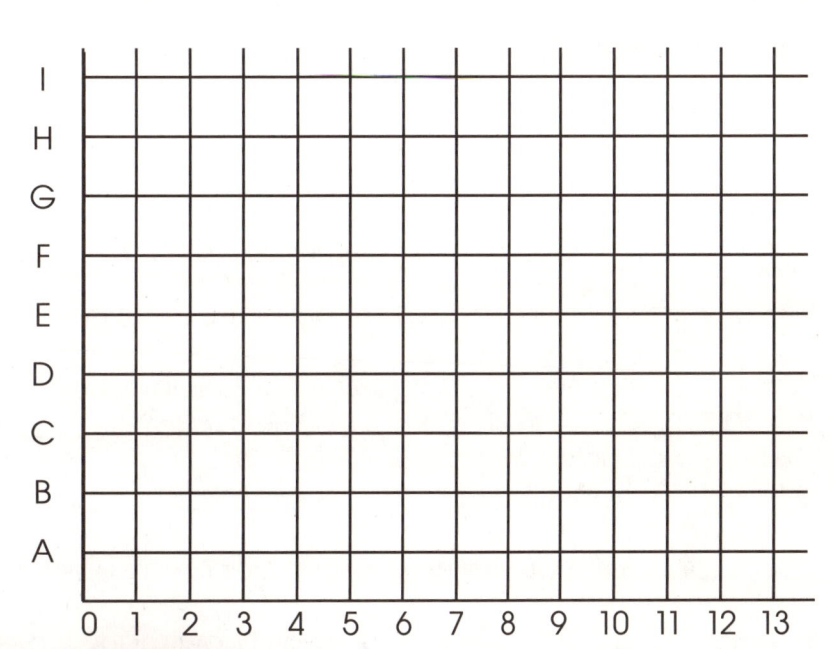

Is her home closer to the bank or the grocery? _____

Does she pass the playground on her way to school? _____

If she needs to stop at the library after school, will she be closer to home or farther away? _____

43

Probability

Directions: Write the probability ratios to answer these questions.

1. Using the spinner shown, what is the probability of spinning a 4? _____

2. Using the spinner shown, what is the chance of not spinning a 2? _____

3. Using the spinner shown, what is the probability of spinning a 6, 7 or 3? _____

4. What is the probability of getting heads or tails when you toss a coin? _____

Directions: Toss a coin 20 times and record the outcome of each toss. Then answer the questions.   _____ Heads _____ Tails

5. What was the ratio of heads to tails in the 20 tosses? _____

6. Was the outcome of getting heads or tails in the 20 tosses the same as the probability ratio? _____

7. Why or why not? _____

The probability ratio of getting any number on a cube of dice is 1:6.

Directions: Toss a die 36 times and record how many times it lands on each number. Then answer the questions.

_____ one   _____ two   _____ three   _____ four   _____ five   _____ six

8. What was the ratio for each number on the die?

_____ one   _____ two   _____ three   _____ four   _____ five   _____ six

9. Did any of the numbers have a ratio close to the actual probability ratio? _____

10. What do the outcomes of flipping a coin and tossing a die tell you about the probability of an event happening?

_____

Send in the Replacements

A thesaurus can help you find synonyms. A **synonym** is a word that has the same or almost the same meaning as another word.

Example:
FIND: *verb* SYN locate, discover, detect, uncover, see, etc.

Directions: Use a thesaurus. Replace each word in bold with a synonym.

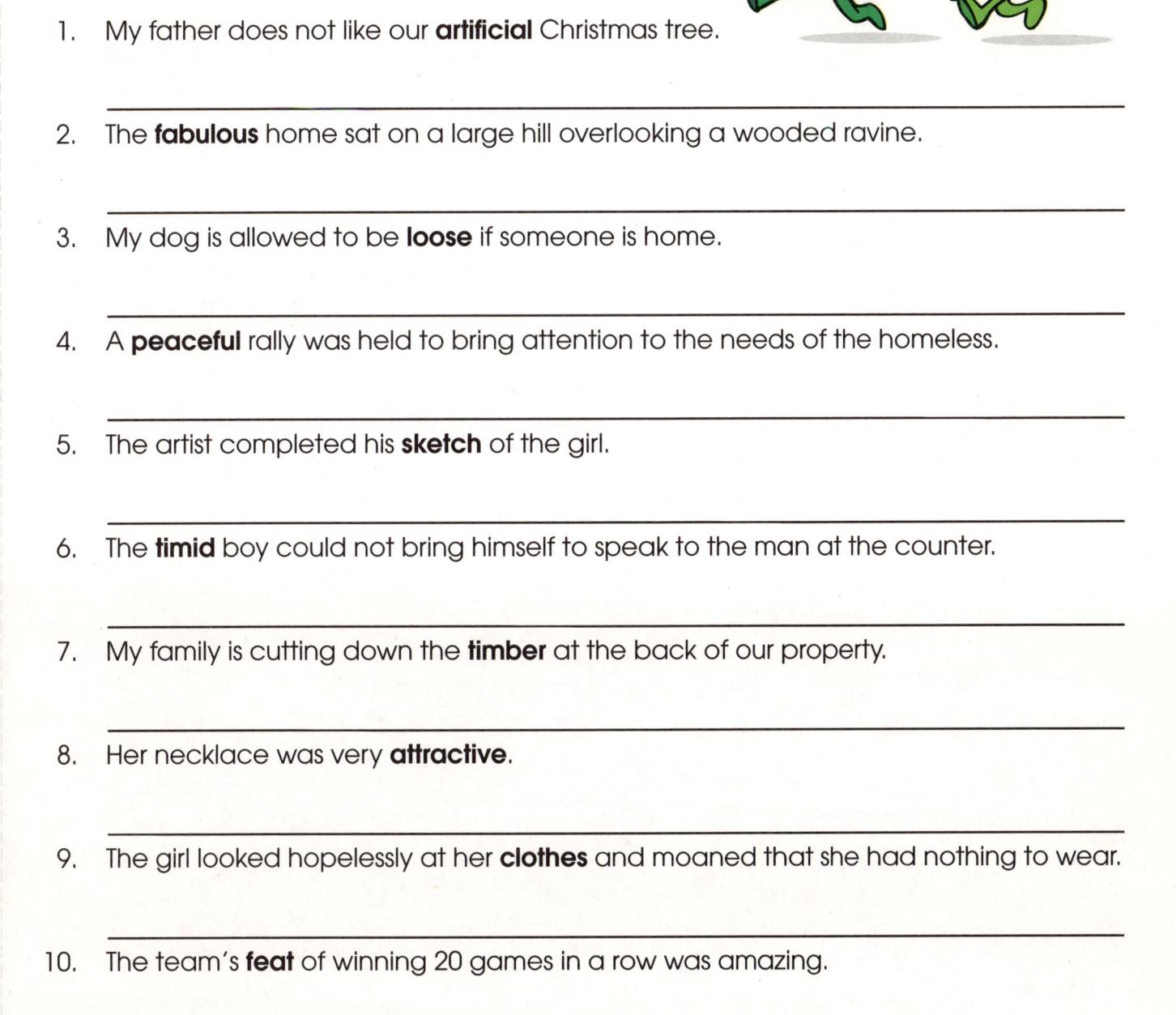

1. My father does not like our **artificial** Christmas tree.

2. The **fabulous** home sat on a large hill overlooking a wooded ravine.

3. My dog is allowed to be **loose** if someone is home.

4. A **peaceful** rally was held to bring attention to the needs of the homeless.

5. The artist completed his **sketch** of the girl.

6. The **timid** boy could not bring himself to speak to the man at the counter.

7. My family is cutting down the **timber** at the back of our property.

8. Her necklace was very **attractive**.

9. The girl looked hopelessly at her **clothes** and moaned that she had nothing to wear.

10. The team's **feat** of winning 20 games in a row was amazing.

Riddle Fun

Directions: Underline the pair of antonyms in each riddle. **Antonyms** are words that have opposite meanings. Then, use the following code to find the answers.

CODE
A = 1, B = 2, C = 3, D = 4, E=5, F=6, G=7, H=8, I=9, J=10, K=11, L=12, M=13, N=14, O=15, P=16, Q=17, R=18, S=19, T=20, U=21, V=22, W=23, X=24, Y=25, Z=26

1. What goes up but never comes down?
   25 15 21 18   1 7 5

2. What is dark yet made by light?
   1   19 8 1 4 15 23

3. What can you hold in your right hand but not in your left?
   25 15 21 18   12 5 6 20   5 12 2 15 23

4. How can you leave a room with two legs and return with six legs?
   3 15 13 5   2 1 3 11   23 9 20 8   1   3 8 1 9 18

5. What goes through a door but never in or out?
   1   11 5 25 8 15 12 5

6. What's the difference between the rising and setting sun?
   1   4 1 25

7. What is the beginning of eternity and the end of time and space?
   20 8 5   12 5 20 20 5 18   5

8. If a farmer raises corn in dry weather, what does he raise in wet weather?
   1 14   21 13 2 18 5 12 12 1

What's the Difference?

Directions: Write the correct homophone from the box next to each definition. Remember, a **homophone** is a word that sounds like another, but has a different meaning. Then, write the boxed letters in order to discover the answer to the riddle below.

Word Box
threw/through
peace/piece
base/bass
colonel/ kernel
scents/cents
brood/brewed
caret/carrot
herd/heard
threw/through
creek/creak
right/rite
vise/vice
hanger/hangar
berry/bury
slay/sleigh
stationery/stationary
wade/weighed
suite/sweet
heir/air
missed/mist

1. military rank
2. odors
3. tossed
4. flock
5. grating noise
6. sled
7. writing paper
8. walk in water
9. sugary
10. successor
11. an orange edible root
12. group of animals
13. put underground
14. tranquility
15. grain of corn
16. fog
17. used for hanging things
18. clamp
19. correct
20. deep voice

What's the difference between someone who parks a car and someone who is smashing dishes?

47

Name _____

Multiple Meanings

Directions: Fill in the bubble next to the correct definition of the bold word in each sentence. The first one has been done for you.

1. Try to **flag** down a car to get us some help!
   - ○ to signal to stop
   - ○ cloth used as symbol

2. We listened to the **band** play the National Anthem.
   - ○ group of musicians
   - ○ a binding or tie

3. He was the **sole** survivor of the plane crash.
   - ○ bottom of the foot
   - ○ one and only

4. I am going to **pound** the nail with this hammer.
   - ○ to hit hard
   - ○ a unit of weight

5. He lived on what little **game** he could find in the woods.
   - ○ animals for hunting
   - ○ form of entertainment

6. We are going to **book** the midnight flight from Miami.
   - ○ to reserve in advance
   - ○ a written work

7. The **pitcher** looked toward first base before throwing the ball.
   - ○ baseball team member
   - ○ container for pouring

8. My grandfather and I played a **game** of checkers last night.
   - ○ animals for hunting
   - ○ form of entertainment

9. They raise the **flag** over City Hall every morning.
   - ○ to signal to stop
   - ○ cloth used as symbol

48

Idioms

An **idiom** is a figure of speech that has a meaning different from the literal one.

Example:

Dad is **in the doghouse** because he was late for dinner.

Meaning: Dad is in trouble because he was late for dinner.

Directions: Write the meanings of the idioms in bold.

1. He was a **bundle of nerves** waiting for his test scores.
   _____

2. It was **raining cats and dogs**.
   _____

3. My friend and I decided to **bury the hatchet** after our argument.
   _____

4. He gave me the **cold shoulder** when I spoke to him.
   _____

5. My mom **blew up** when she saw my poor report card.
   _____

6. I was **on pins and needles** before my skating performance.
   _____

7. When the student didn't answer, the teacher asked, "**Did the cat get your tongue**?"
   _____

8. The city **rolled out the red carpet** for the returning Olympic champion.
   _____

9. They hired a clown for the young boy's birthday party to help **break the ice**.
   _____

Pick the Prefix

A **prefix** is a group of letters added to the beginning of a word. When a prefix is added, the meaning of the word is changed. Here are some prefixes and their meanings.

Prefix	Meaning
un	not, opposite of
re	again, back
in	not
dis	not, lack of

Directions: Read the report. Figure out which prefix from the box goes in front of each underlined word. Write these prefixes in the space provided.

During the American Revolution, many soldiers were _____ happy. Some had never been away from home before, and they were _____ satisfied with how they had to live. But the cause was important to them, so they tried not to be _____ couraged.

The Battle of Bunker Hill was the first great battle of the American Revolution. The American Army had to _____ treat. The soldiers may have lost the battle, but the difference between the number of soldiers on each side was greatly _____ fair. In addition, the British army had better weapons and what seemed like _____ destructible powers. However, now the American Patriots were determined and _____ stoppable. During battles, their aim may have sometimes been _____ accurate. Nevertheless, they began to _____ gain their strength.

Eventually, under the leadership of General George Washington, the American army overcame its _____ advantage and won the war. Had it not been for the bravery of these largely _____ trained soldiers, the United States may never have been born.

50

Find the Suffix

Suffixes are word parts added to the endings of words. When you add a suffix to a word, its meaning as well as its part of speech is changed. Also, sometimes the spelling changes.

Directions: Read each sentence. Change each underlined word by adding the suffix **ful, ible,** or **ly.** Write the new word on the line.

1. Mark and his dog headed toward the cave quick. _____

2. The play dog ran ahead. _____

3. As they neared the entrance, the boy was hope about what they would find. _____

4. The dog eager waited while the boy looked over the area. _____

5. Mark knew the sense thing was to turn around. _____

6. He wondered if their walk through the cave would go smooth. _____

7. He hoped nothing horror would happen. _____

8. They would have to be flex enough to get around all the curves. _____

9. Sudden, there was a loud noise. _____

10. Mark and his dog jumped when they heard the noise and ran rapid toward home. _____

Hunt for Roots

Directions: The words in the box have Latin and Greek roots. Find the words from the box in the puzzle. Look across, down, backward, and diagonally. Circle the words.

Word box:
- thermometer
- autobiography
- telescope
- astronaut
- autograph
- paragraph
- hemisphere
- centipede
- fortune
- graph

```
P A R A G R A P H T H
C R D C Y H U R S E E
E T B E N U T R O F M
N H H T G R O P E A I
T E Y P R E B P E S S
I R D L A A I P E T P
P M E A P R O P Q R H
E O Z U H C G T L O E
D M N D S R R O T N R
E E T B U A E T A E
W T L E R E P G R U P
T E A V T L H D A T A
T R E N J P Y U C T O
```

Directions: Write each word you circled above next to its definition below.

1. a famous person's signature _____
2. an insect with one hundred legs _____
3. part of a composition _____
4. an instrument that tells the temperature _____
5. explorer in space _____
6. a book someone writes about his or her life _____
7. an instrument used to study the sky _____
8. half the world _____
9. a diagram that compares things _____
10. a lot of money _____

Digraphs

A **digraph** is two consonants pronounced as one sound.

Examples: sh as in **shell**, **ch** as in **chew**, **th** as in **thin**

Directions: Write **sh**, **ch** or **th** to complete each word below.

1. ____ reaten
2. ____ ill
3. ____ ock
4. ____ iver
5. ____ aw
6. ____ allenge
7. peri ____
8. ____ ield
9. ____ art
10. ____ rive

Directions: Complete these sentences with a word, or form of the word, from the list above.

1. A trip to the South Pole would really be a (**ch**) _____ .

2. The ice there never (**th**) _____ because the temperature averages –50°C.

3. How can any living thing (**th**) _____ or even live when it's so cold?

4. With 6 months of total darkness and those icy temperatures, any plants would soon (**sh**) _____ .

5. Even the thought of that numbing cold makes me (**sh**) _____ .

6. The cold and darkness (**th**) _____ the lives of explorers.

7. The explorers take along maps and (**ch**) _____ to help them find their way.

8. Special clothing helps protect and (**sh**) _____ them from the cold.

9. Still, the weather must be a (**sh**) _____ at first.

10. Did someone leave a door open? Suddenly I feel a (**ch**) _____ .

Subjects and Verbs

Directions: Underline the subject and verb in each sentence below. Write **S** over the subject and **V** over the verb. If the verb is two words, mark them both.

                S   V   V
Examples: Dennis was drinking some punch.

                    S   V
            The punch was too sweet.

1. Hayley brags about her dog all the time.

2. Mrs. Thomas scrubbed the dirt off her car.

3. Then her son rinsed off the soap.

4. The teacher was flipping through the cards.

5. Jenny's rabbit was hungry and thirsty.

6. Your science report lacks a little detail.

7. Chris is stocking the shelves with cans of soup.

8. The accident caused a huge dent in our car.

Just as sentences can have two subjects, they can also have two verbs.

                S   S   V   V
Example: Jennifer and Amie fed the dog and gave him clean water.

Directions: Underline all the subjects and verbs in these sentences. Write **S** over the subjects and **V** over the verbs.

1. Mom and Dad scrubbed and rinsed the basement floor.

2. The men came and stocked the lake with fish.

3. Someone broke the window and ran away.

4. Carrie punched a hole in the paper and threaded yarn through the hole.

5. Julie and Pat turned their bikes around and went home.

Picture This!

A **compound word** is formed by two or more words.
Some compound words are written as one word.
Examples: blueberry   motorcycle

Other compound words are joined by a hyphen.
Examples: twenty-one   editor-in-chief

Directions: Write the compound word for each of the following cartoons.

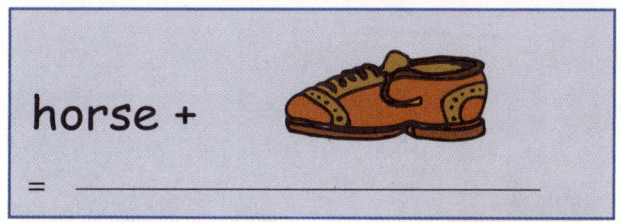

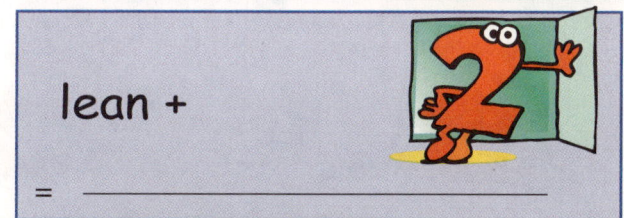

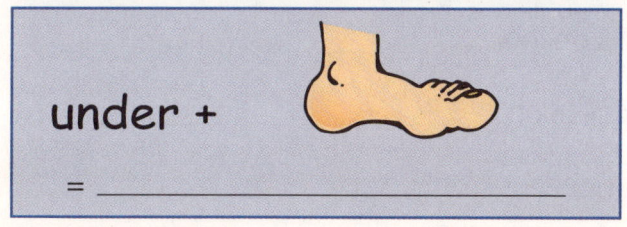

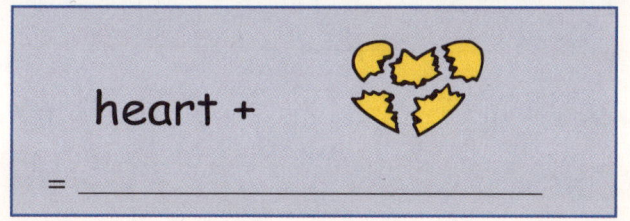

[shell] + fish
= _____

steam + [rowboat]
= _____

[3] + story
= _____

[bull] +frog
= _____

[cup] + board
= _____

horse + [shoes]
= _____

[kite] +flying
= _____

lean + [2 going out door]
= _____

tea + [spoon]
= _____

[calendars] + round
= _____

under + [foot]
= _____

heart + [broken pieces]
= _____

55

Dividing Words

A **syllable** is a unit of sound in a word. Every syllable has only one vowel sound. The following are some rules of syllables.

> Use hyphens (-) to divide words.
>
> A one-syllable word is never divided.
>
> When a word has a prefix, divide the word between the prefix and the base word.
>
> **Example:** repaint → re-paint
>
> When a word has a suffix with a vowel sound in it, divide the word between the base word and the suffix.
>
> **Example:** cupful → cup-ful
>
> When two or more consonants come between two vowels in a word, the word is usually divided between the first two consonants.
>
> **Example:** surprise → sur-prise
>
> Divide a compound word between the words that make up the compound word.
>
> **Example:** airplane → air-plane
>
> When a vowel is sounded alone in a word, it forms a syllable by itself.
>
> **Example:** monument → mon-u-ment

Directions: Divide the words into syllables. Use the syllable rules to help you.

1. sapwood _____
2. dabble _____
3. freeze _____
4. disclaimer _____
5. hysterical _____

6. millionaire _____
7. questionable _____
8. occupation _____
9. expression _____
10. pavement _____

56

Singular or Plural

A **singular noun** names one person, place, or thing. A **plural noun** names more than one person, place, or thing.

Directions: First read the rules for making plural nouns. Write the plural for each verb listed at the bottom of the page.

For regular nouns:

- Add **s** to most singular nouns to make them plural: dog/dogs, restaurant/restaurants, crayon/crayons.
- If a word ends in **s, sh, ch,** or **x,** add **es** to make it plural: class/classes, beach/beaches, fox/foxes.
- If a noun ends in a **consonant** and **y,** change the **y** to **i** and add **es:** party/parties, jelly/jellies, lady/ladies.

For irregular nouns:

- Some nouns have the same singular and plural form: fish/fish, deer/deer.
- Some nouns change spelling completely when they become plural: child/children, goose/geese.
- Some nouns that end in **f** or **fe** can be made plural by replacing the **f** or **fe** with **v** and adding **es:** leaf/leaves, wife/wives.
- Other nouns that end in **f** can be made plural simply by adding **s:** chief/chiefs, oaf/oafs.
- If a noun ends in a consonant followed by **o,** check the dictionary to find out the plural form. Some end in **s** and some end in **es:** cello/cellos, tomato/tomatoes.

1. wolf _____
2. cheese _____
3. baby _____
4. buffalo _____
5. Walsh _____
6. idea _____
7. knife _____
8. piano _____
9. jetty _____
10. galosh _____
11. Johnson _____
12. bus _____
13. county _____
14. sandwich _____
15. sheriff _____
16. life _____

The Plural Surprise

Remember to add **es** to nouns that end in **ch, s, sh, ss, x,** or **z.**

Directions: Change each word to a plural by adding **s** or **es**. Write the plural of the word on the space provided.

decoration _____   other _____

branch _____   chip _____

noise _____   box _____

guess _____   plate _____

Directions: Write the plural nouns from above on each blank to complete the story.

Jake could not remember when he was supposed to be at Peter's house. He decided to walk over to see what was happening.

When he saw the front yard, he knew something wasn't right. He saw balloons that needed to be blown up by the bushes in front of the house. There were also _____ with other _____. These needed to be hung from tree _____ as well.

The back door was open and Jake walked in. On the kitchen table were _____ and dip, and other food. There were _____, glasses, and utensils spread out on the table. Jake knew something was not right. _____ were coming from the other room. He heard a vacuum cleaner and people talking.

Jake wondered what to do. Just then, three friends walked in. "You're early!" exclaimed Peter.

"Surprise," said the _____.
"You get three _____ about what's going on here."

"Since today is my birthday, I only need one guess. You're having a party for me," said Jake.

58

The Art Exhibit

A **verb phrase** consists of one **main verb** and one or more **helping verbs.** The main verb is the most important verb in a verb phrase.

Directions: The following is a list of quotes overheard at Lincoln School's Fall Art Exhibit. Find the verb phrase in each quote. Then, circle the main verb and underline the helping verbs. The first one has been done for you.

1. "Who <u>could have</u> (drawn) that picture?"

2. "Bobby must have been the artist. He has been drawing since the third grade."

3. "The art department said that they will be organizing another exhibit soon."

4. "I am going to draw something for the next exhibit."

5. "Eric will show his painting, too. He has been working on it for the past few weeks."

6. "Any student can be considered for one of the exhibits. But only the best work is shown."

7. "We must not bring food or drinks to the room; if someone spilled, the artwork could be ruined."

8. "That's Mr. Franklin, the art teacher. He will be showing off the artwork once everyone is here."

9. "You will recognize many of the artists' names."

10. "This is the best exhibit the school has put on in two years!"

As a Matter of Fact . . .

An **adjective** is a word that describes a noun or a pronoun. It answers questions such as which one, how many, or what kind?

Directions: Read the facts below. Circle each adjective and draw an arrow to the noun it describes. Then, write the adjective where it belongs on the chart.

1. The "red eye" is not a terrible disease but an overnight flight.
2. The human body contains eight pints of blood.
3. A bald eagle is not really bald; it has white feathers on its head.
4. The imaginary lines that mark the time zones are called meridians.
5. At night, sea otters wrap themselves in beds of kelp, a type of large seaweed, so the currents do not take them out to sea.
6. On a ship, the day is divided into five watches of four hours each and two watches of two hours each.
7. Among those astronauts who walked on the Moon, Neil Armstrong was first.
8. The eye of the giant squid is reported to be up to 15 inches across.

How Many?	What Kind Of?	Which One?

What's Missing?

Adverbs are words that describe or modify verbs, adjectives, or other adverbs. They answer questions like **when? where? how? how much?**

Directions: Write the correct adverb in each sentence. Use the words in the box. Time yourself. Can you do it in four minutes?

closely	quite
instantly	carefully
thoroughly	easily
rather	mainly
suddenly	rarely

1. The detectives _____ searched the crime scene for clues.

2. Just glancing at my mother's face, I knew _____ that she was upset about something.

3. After working for eight hours we were _____ tired.

4. No one knows what to wear because the weather has been _____ unpredictable.

5. My father has _____ if ever been late to work, even though he commutes over an hour each morning.

6. The storm hit _____, leaving many unsuspecting residents stranded.

7. My brother is _____ interested in music and spends most of his spare time playing his guitar.

8. I _____ rechecked my calculations to make sure I hadn't made any mistakes.

9. Some people confuse me with my sister because we _____ resemble each other.

10. We _____ finished the test in no time at all.

61

Contraction Action

It's and **its** sound the same, but they have different spellings and meanings. **It's** is a contraction that means **it is**. **Its** means **belonging to**.

Directions: Marla and Darla opened an ice cream parlor. Here's a conversation they had on their first day in business. Write **it's** or **its** to correctly complete each sentence.

1. I hope _____ a busy day with lots of customers.

2. The store is on a good street. _____ location is perfect.

3. _____ going to be a success because of the unusual flavors we offer.

4. Summer is coming. _____ going to be a busy time for us.

5. _____ time to unlock the door.

6. I love the bell on the door. _____ sound will ring each time someone comes in.

7. Remember to use the newest scoop. _____ handle is blue.

8. We can't forget to thank everyone. _____ important to be polite.

9. _____ cozy feeling will bring everyone back for more.

Directions: Combine each pronoun with verbs from the box to form contractions. See how many contractions you can make.

will	had	have	am	are	is

1. I _____
2. she _____
3. he _____
4. we _____
5. they _____

Name _____

The Babysitter's List

The, an and **a** are called **articles.** Articles are a special kind of adjective.

The is always used to refer to a specific noun, so it is called a **definite article.**

A and **an** refer to any noun, so they are called **indefinite articles.**

Directions: Help Mrs. Farkle complete the list of instructions she made for the babysitter. Write the correct article on the line in each sentence.

1. We'll be at _____ Golden Dragon Restaurant until 8:00.

   We are going to _____ movies after dinner.

2. You can make _____ simple dinner.

3. There is pizza in _____ freezer.

   There is also fruit in _____ bowl on the table.

4. Have _____ kids use paper plates.

   Otherwise, they'll make _____ huge mess!

5. For dessert each child can have _____ apple.

6. There are emergency phone numbers near _____ kitchen phone.

7. The kids can watch _____ video if they want.

8. Read _____ book to _____ kids at bedtime.

9. Please do not talk on _____ phone for longer than five minutes.

10. If you watch TV after the kids go to bed, keep _____ volume low.

11. You can have _____ snack whenever you want!

Is That a Fact?

A **preposition** is a word that shows how one word is related to another in a sentence.

A **prepositional phrase** is a group of words that begins with a preposition and ends with a noun or pronoun.

Directions: Each fact below is missing a prepositional phrase. Use the code to figure out each one. Write the phrase on each line.

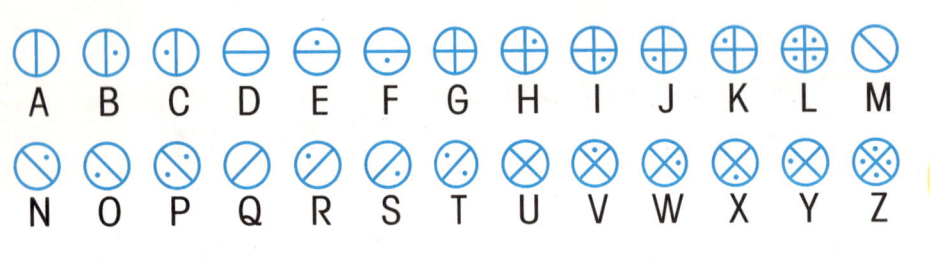

A B C D E F G H I J K L M
N O P Q R S T U V W X Y Z

1. The Iditarod is a 1200-mile dogsled race

_____

2. Air rushes _____

   at 100 miles per hour when you sneeze.

_____

3. Red is the most commonly found color

_____

4. The Islands of Hawaii evolved as volcanoes erupted

_____

5. French fries are not really _____ _____ but

   _____ _____

_____

6. Bertrand Piccard and Brian Jones were the first to fly _____

   _____ nonstop _____ _____

_____

The Conjunction Code

Conjunctions are words that join other words, phrases, and sentences.

Directions: Use the conjunctions from the word box to complete the sentences below. Two conjunctions are used twice.

unless	because	whether	either
if	when	after	while	or
nor	before	and	once

1. _____ you study for your test, I'm going to finish my math homework.
2. _____ you stay _____ go is completely up to you.
3. We can't go swimming yet, _____ the surf is too rough.
4. We were just about to eat _____ the phone rang.
5. We aren't going _____ you can go, too.
6. Neither my brother _____ my sister wants to practice right now.
7. We have both math _____ English homework tonight.
8. _____ we hear anything, we'll call you immediately.
9. We have to straighten up our room _____ we can come over.
10. _____ we plan a picnic, it always rains.
11. I ran as fast as I could _____ I didn't want to miss the bus.
12. We will _____ go to the mall _____ to a movie tonight.
13. _____ I return this book to the library, I have to stop at the store.

65

Name _____

All About You

Directions: Fill in the blanks so each sentence tells something about you. Add commas and periods where they belong. Then, label each sentence **simple**, **compound**, or **complex**.

1. _____ Hi! My name is _____

2. _____ There are _____ people in my family and I _____

3. _____ We've lived here in _____ ever since _____

4. _____ I attend _____ and _____

5. _____ My favorite class is _____ although I _____

6. _____ I hope to become _____ when I _____

7. _____ Sometimes I _____ when _____ because _____

8. _____ I always _____ before _____

9. _____ Even though _____ I'd like _____

10. _____ As soon as I _____

66

The List

Underline titles of books, magazines, works of art, plays, movies, television shows, and names of ships and planes. Use quotation marks around titles of chapters, short stories, short poems, and songs.

Directions: Here's Miss Muffet's list of the Top Ten Things to Do While on Vacation. The little Miss's list has a few errors, though. Help her out by underlining and adding quotation marks to titles and names as necessary.

1. Practice my dramatic reading of The Spider and the Fly for my appearance on Star Search.

2. Rent the movie of E.B. White's Charlotte's Web.

3. Record my rock version of Eensy Weensy Spider and send to the Backstreet Boys.

4. Finish my article, How to Live With Spiders and Like It, for Ranger Rick.

5. Go for a ride on the Out to Sea, my friend Bobby Shafto's private yacht.

6. Read the chapter Major Order of Arachnids in Kids' Guide to Insects & Spiders.

7. Get tickets for Tarantella, the new Broadway musical that everyone's talking about.

8. Arrange for a screen test for a possible role in the sequel to Arachnophobia.

Game Show Contestants

Sometimes you need to **infer**, or make an educated guess, about information that is missing from a selection. Use details from the selection and your own experience to make inferences.

Directions: Read the story. Then use story details to infer the identity of each contestant. Write each contestant's name on the line below the correct picture.

_____   _____   _____

_____   _____   _____

The two teams were preparing for the game show to start. On the first team, Nellie was busy reciting math formulas backwards and forwards. Jill was doing push-ups at the front of the stage to calm her nerves. Vinnie chimed in, "Hey, are you doing push-ups? This is a game to test how smart you are, not how strong... but then, what do you care, you already have the smartest kid in school on your team! Did I tell you about the time my sister was on a game show? She...."

Vinnie kept talking but no one was really listening. Gary had his hands full putting plastic spiders under Sam's chair, hoping he might distract Sam when it was his turn to answer a question. Sam didn't know about the spiders, but he looked like he was about to cry anyway; he hated having to sit on the stage and speak in front of a group of people. He was especially worried because his team was still missing a contestant, Lena, who was always late.

Finally, Lena arrived and Vinnie started to complain. "Lena, how is our team supposed to win if you can't even show up on time? I was just saying to my best friend the other day that . . ."

Lena interrupted him. "Stick a sock in it, Vinnie, or I'll steal your lunch money like I did last week."

68

Why Write?

There are four main purposes for writing: to **inform**, to **entertain**, to **persuade**, and to **express** feelings, opinions, or beliefs.

Directions: Think about the writing that you have read. Then, decide whether each of the following statements is true or false. Follow the directions.

1. Writers can only write for one purpose at a time.
   If true, circle the letter in box # 16.
   If false, circle the letter in box # 18.

2. Informative writing is always the most fun to read.
   If true, circle the letter in box # 14.
   If false, circle the letter in box # 4.

3. Writers who write to inform their readers don't ever try to write to entertain.
   If true, circle the letter in box # 25.
   If false, circle the letter in box # 12.

4. Writers who write to inform include many facts in their work.
   If true, circle the letter in box # 20.
   If false, circle the letter in box # 3.

5. Writers who write to inform should never express opinions in their work.
   If true, circle the letter in box # 8.
   If false, circle the letter in box # 1.

6. Good persuasive writers also provide information on their topics.
   If true, circle the letter in box # 7.
   If false, circle the letter in box # 21.

7. It is easier to write to entertain people than it is to write to inform them.
   If true, circle the letter in box # 15.
   If false, circle the letter in box # 11.

8. When writers write to inform their readers, they can also entertain them with interesting facts and stories.
   If true, circle the letter in box # 22.
   If false, circle the letter in box # 5.

9. A story about a struggle with illness is a good example of writing with a main purpose of expressing feelings, opinions, or beliefs.
   If true, circle the letter in box # 10. If false, circle the letter in box # 29.

1	2	3	4	5
E	A	T	X	N
6	7	8	9	10
H	C	S	M	E
11	12	13	14	15
L	L	R	A	I
16	17	18	19	20
V	B	E	D	N
21	22	23	24	25
U	T	R	O	G

Now, write all the circled letters, in order, to complete this sentence:

If you set your mind to it, you can be an ☐☐☐☐☐☐☐☐ writer!

What's the Main Idea?

Often the main idea of a passage is **stated** in a sentence. Sometimes, however, you have to figure out the **unstated** main idea by looking at important details.

Directions: Read each paragraph. Then, write a sentence that states the main idea for each paragraph.

One of the most popular forms of entertainment today is playing computer games. Children are fascinated by these games. They are popular because they have exciting graphics, fun activities, and a wide variety of games.

Stated Main Idea: _____

_____

Some radio stations play jazz. Others play rock. Still others play country. Some stations just report the news and weather. What a lot of variety we get from radio!

Unstated Main Idea: _____

_____

Do you have a hobby? One kind of hobby involves collecting things. Some people collect stamps. Others may collect dolls or stuffed animals. Many people collect and trade sports cards. Another kind of hobby involves building things. Some people build models of ships and airplanes from kits or build large structures from Legos. Other hobbies involve music, art, dance, and sports.

Unstated Main Idea: _____

_____

Name _____

Compare! Contrast! Choose!

Directions: Kobe wants to buy a bike and has saved $125. He found some information about one bike from a company online. He also cut out an ad from the newspaper for a similar bike. Help Kobe compare and contrast the two bikes. Complete the chart.

Rally Boy's Mountain Master

When it comes to bicycles for active, hard-playing boys, ages 10-14, sturdiness and safety are essential. This yellow and black 24" wheel Mountain Master offers both and is sure to please both parents and kids. It features a unique oversized frame that makes getting on and off a snap, a large derailleur guard, alloy hubs and rims, and many other dependable components. A 21-speed drive train makes riding effortless. The twist shifters come equipped with an easy-to-read gear display to let you know what gear you're in. Top-notch linear pull brakes allow young riders to stop when they need to. The 1.95-inch all-terrain tires perform well on any surface. Your cost is only $229.99.*

*Price does not include shipping. Delivery 4-5 working days. Assembly required.

FOR SALE
Used boy's 24" blue Rally Mountain King bike 21-speed, easy-to-read gear shift display, pull brakes, large derailleur guard and an extra set of 1.95 all-terrain tires. Just a year old, still like new. Perfect for a 10- to 14-year-old boy. Come and check it out. Take it for a spin around the block. Asking only $100. Call 555-1234 for more details.

Compare

_____   _____
_____   _____

Contrast

_____   _____
_____   _____
_____   _____
_____   _____
_____   _____

If you were Kobe, which bike would you buy? Why?
_____
_____

What a Character!

Directions: Who is your favorite TV character? List words to describe the character on the left side of the Venn diagram. Do the same for your favorite character from a book, listing his or her traits on the right. Make sure that any traits the two share are listed in the middle. Then, answer the questions at the bottom of the page.

Favorite TV Character: _____   Favorite Book Character: _____

Show: _____   Book title: _____

Show   **Book**

Alike

1. What is your favorite TV character's most unusual trait? _____
_____
_____

2. What is your favorite book character's most unusual trait? _____
_____
_____

Name _____

Plot Out the Action

The **plot** is the main storyline in any work of fiction. The most important parts of a plot are:

background: the introduction; what the reader needs to know about the characters and the general situation	conflict: the problem that the main character/characters must solve or the goal that he/she/they want to achieve	rising action: what the characters do to overcome the conflict; this may include encountering more problems	climax: usually the most exciting part of the story, often when character(s) must resolve the conflict	falling action: events that occur after the conflict has been resolved

Directions: Read this story about Luis. Then, answer the questions at the bottom of the page. Make sure to use complete sentences.

Luis' mom needed his help. She was planning a backyard party for his grandmother. She was so busy getting the house ready, she needed someone to help her do the shopping. She gave Luis her shopping list and $40.

Luis had been to the store many times before but never by himself. He got a cart and walked up the first aisle. As he put each item in the cart, he crossed it off the list.

While he was in the snacks aisle, he decided to add some things to the cart. His mom had only written pretzels on the list, but he put potato chips and popcorn in the cart, too. In the drink section, Luis added orange drinks and root beer.

When he got to the checkout, the cashier told him that the total was $47.25. But Luis only had $40. He couldn't believe his mother hadn't given him enough money! Then, he remembered that he had put extra things in the cart. He asked the cashier if he could put some of his items back. When she told him yes, he gave back the extra snacks and drinks. By doing this, he brought the total down to $38.

When Luis arrived home with the groceries, he unpacked them and told his mom what had happened. She thanked him and told him that next time he went to the grocery store, she would give him some extra money. That way he could choose something special to buy as a reward for helping her out!

1. Give the background for this story. _____

_____

2. What is the main conflict in this story? _____

_____

3. Describe the rising action of the story. _____

_____

_____

_____

So Much Fiction!

Directions: Read about the different types of fiction. Then, label each book description below with the correct type of fiction.

Realistic fiction has characters and events like those in real life. It is set in a place that is or seems real.

Fantasy is about impossible events and is often set in an unreal world.

Science fiction is fantasy based on science. It often takes place in the future and sometimes in outer space.

A **mystery** may seem realistic. Its plot is based on a puzzle that the main characters (and reader) try to solve.

A **fable** is a short story that teaches a lesson. Its characters are often animals.

A **folktale** was first told aloud and was handed down from generation to generation. It may explain how some feature of nature came to exist.

1. _____

Have Space Suit, Will Travel
by Robert Heinlein

Kip Russell is in the backyard of his house when he is kidnapped by the Mother Thing and taken to the moon. He travels to Luna and the Magellenic cloud—and learns he must help save the Earth.

2. _____

The Story of the Milky Way: A Cherokee Tale
by Joseph Bruchac, illustrated by Virginia A. Stroud

Villagers cleverly frighten away a thieving spirit dog. As it leaps into the sky, grains of stolen cornmeal fall from its mouth and become stars.

3. _____

Mandie and the Secret Tunnel
by Lois Gladys Leppard

It is the year 1900, and Mandie is searching her dead uncle's mansion for a missing will when she finds a secret tunnel and strangers who claim to be relatives. But can they help her with her search?

4. _____

Beezus and Ramona
by Beverly Cleary

Beezus wishes she could love her little sister, Ramona. But Ramona keeps doing things to make Beezus just furious!

5. _____

The Little Red Ant and the Great Big Crumb
by Shirley Climo, illustrated by Francisco X. Mora

A small red ant finds a delicious crumb in a Mexican cornfield. She asks many animals to help her move it, but finally she learns a lesson about who is the strongest of all.

6. _____

Harry Potter and the Prisoner of Azkaban
by J.K. Rowling

It is vacation and Harry runs away from his uncle's house because he has accidentally caused horrible Aunt Marge to turn into a drifting balloon. He thinks he's safe when a purple bus carries him off, but his dangerous adventures have just begun.

Name _____

Sort and Shelve

Directions: Read about the different types of nonfiction. Then, look at the books shown below. On the line underneath each book, write the type of nonfiction it is.

An **informational book** gives facts about a topic and may contain the writer's opinions.

A **how-to book** gives directions for an activity.

A **reference book** presents a specialized type of information in a very organized way.

A **textbook** presents facts in one subject area and often gives a broad general view of the subject. It does not contain opinions.

A **biography** is the true story of someone's life, written by someone else.

An **autobiography** is the true story of the writer's life up to that time.

A **personal narrative** focuses on an important event in the writer's life.

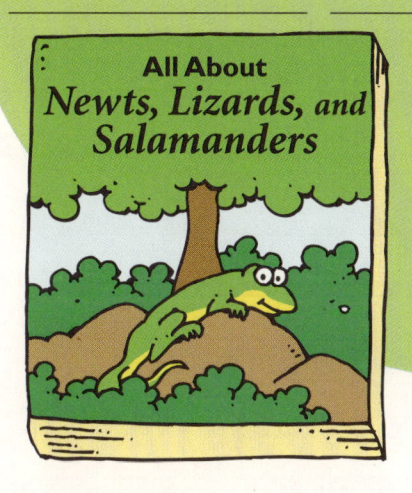

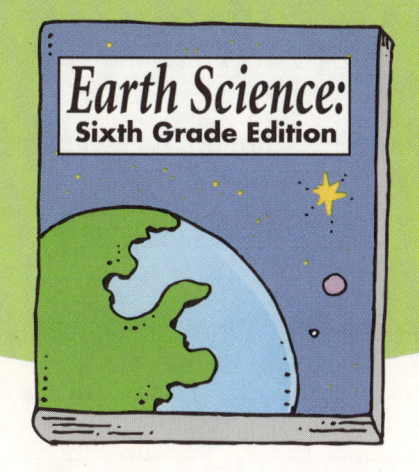

Castaway! My Year on a Desert Island

The Life and Times of Florence Nightingale

The Journal of Benjamin Franklin

International Atlas

All About Newts, Lizards, and Salamanders

Earth Science: Sixth Grade Edition

Nine Treehouses You Can Build

75

The Missing Painting

Directions: Read the following mystery and answer the questions.

Detective Doolittle couldn't sleep. He was puzzled by the facts of his latest case. A priceless painting had been reported stolen from the home of Neptune Island's wealthiest resident, Eloise Rappaport. He didn't find any evidence and there were no witnesses, either. Who could have sneaked into the Rappaport home in broad daylight and stolen a painting the size of a refrigerator? It just didn't seem possible.

The next day, Detective Doolittle drove back to the crime scene. Miss Rappaport let him in and took him to the library where the robbery had taken place.

"So tell me again, in your own words, what happened," said Doolittle.

"Well," said Miss Rappaport, "It was Saturday afternoon and it was very hot—you know, usual July weather. I had just come back from lunch at my friend Marcia's house when I noticed that the library door was open. It was around 2:30. I didn't think much of it so I went upstairs to change for the cocktail party I was to go to that night. When I came back downstairs, I heard the phone ringing. I went to pick up the extension in the library—that's when I noticed that my painting was missing!"

"And you didn't see or hear anything strange that day?" the detective asked.

"No, but there is something that's been bothering me. At the time I didn't think anything of it but I saw my neighbor, Fred, on his way into the Post Office the very next day with a giant box, big enough to fit my painting in, marked 'Fragile.' I offered to give him a ride home but he acted really strange and ran away. I've always though he was a weird fellow."

"Hmmm …" said Detective Doolittle. He was frustrated; he'd never had so much trouble cracking a case before. Something about Miss Rappaport's story was troubling him. "Thanks for your help. I'll be going now. Just one more question—who was on the phone when you took that call in the library that day?"

"Oh," she said, "it was the gardener, Theresa. She was calling to tell me she wouldn't be in that day because she had to drive her daughter to kindergarten. I'll tell you, she has been trouble since I hired her last summer. I wouldn't be surprised if she was the one who took the painting!"

"Maybe she did, Miss Rappaport," said Detective Doolittle angrily, "but you're the one who's lying!"

1. Why does Detective Doolittle say that Miss Rappaport is lying? _____

_____

_____

2. What do you think happened to the painting? What makes you think so? _____

_____

3. On another sheet of paper, write a conclusion to the story.

Fact or Opinion?

What is the difference between a fact and an opinion? **Facts** can be proven true. **Opinions** are beliefs, judgments, or feelings that cannot be verified.

Directions: Each of the following sentences contains a fact and an opinion. Underline the part that states a fact, and put brackets around each part that states an opinion.

1. [The most exciting place to tour in Washington, D.C. is the White House], which has been the home and office of every U.S. President except George Washington.

2. The capital was named after George Washington, our nation's first President [and the greatest general in our nation's history].

3. The Washington Monument is a 555-foot white marble obelisk [that is enjoyed by every visitor to our nation's capital].

4. [I think the Declaration of Independence, the Constitution, and the Bill of Rights are our nation's most important historic documents], and they are on display at the National Archives.

5. The National Air and Space Museum is one of the Smithsonian Institution's 14 museums [and the most interesting one of all].

6. The National Zoo is also part of the Smithsonian, [and it's a terrific place for families to visit].

7. [The Lincoln Memorial is a beautiful monument], and it includes a gigantic statue of Abraham Lincoln, our 16th President.

8. The dome of the Capitol is visible from many parts of the city [and is a spectacular sight].

9. There is an exhibit for children over eight years old at the U.S. Holocaust Memorial Museum called Daniel's Story, [but I think everyone should see it].

10. The National Gallery of Art, located on the Mall, [is without a doubt the world's greatest art museum].

Report-a-Sauras, Part 1

Directions: You are writing a report about dinosaurs. In each paragraph, you want to answer a certain research question. The following is a list of notes you took at the library. Write each piece of information under the paragraph it goes with.

- Dinosaurs roamed the earth for more than 180 million years, but they became extinct over 65 million years ago.
- By studying fossils, paleontologists can learn about the sizes of the different dinosaurs.
- Almost everything we know about dinosaurs comes from looking at fossils.
- Scientists who study dinosaur fossils are called paleontologists.
- Before paleontologists can study fossils, they must dig them from the ground and clean them very carefully.
- Then, the fossils can be taken to a university or museum and studied.
- By studying fossils, paleontologists can learn what the different types of dinosaurs ate.
- Fossils were formed from dinosaurs when their remains hardened into stone or were surrounded by mud or sand that hardened into stone.
- Fossils are formed over long periods of time from the bones, eggs, and other remains of dinosaurs.
- By studying fossils, paleontologists can learn how the different types of dinosaurs cared for their young.

First paragraph: When did the dinosaurs live?

_____
_____

Second paragraph: What are fossils, and why are they important?

_____
_____
_____
_____
_____
_____

Name _____

Report-a-Sauras, Part 2

Directions: Continue to write each piece of information from page 78 under the paragraph it goes with.

Third paragraph: What are paleontologists, and what do they do?

_____
_____
_____
_____
_____
_____
_____
_____
_____

Fourth paragraph: What can paleontologists learn from looking at fossils?

_____
_____
_____
_____
_____
_____
_____
_____
_____

Proofreading Puzzler

Directions: Proofread the following article for capitalization, punctuation, grammar, and spelling mistakes. Use the proofreading symbols below to mark any mistakes you find.

℘ delete	# space	ꞵ lowercase
∧ insert	b̲ capitalize	¶ new paragraph
a⁀e transpose		

What do a Saint Bernard, a Chihuahua, and a german Shepherd have in common? That's easy—they are all dogs! But why don't all dogs look alike Most terriers are small and low to the ground. Long ago, terriers were used to hunt rats and badgers. The dogs would follow the rats and badgers into their underground homes. Terriers are good diggers there small size helps them get into tight places.

Greyhounds are racing dogs. They run very fast. a greyhound's long legs help it run? Another part of this dog's body that helps it run is its lungs. Just look at the greyhound's large chest! This dog's lungs is large and can hold a lot of air.

Similes Are Like Metaphors

Using **similes** and **metaphors** makes writing interesting. They are ways of describing things.

Similes are comparisons that use **like** or **as**.

Examples: She looked like a frightened mouse.
　　　　　　She looked as frightened as a mouse.

Metaphors are direct comparisons that **do not use like** or **as**.

Example: She was a frightened mouse.

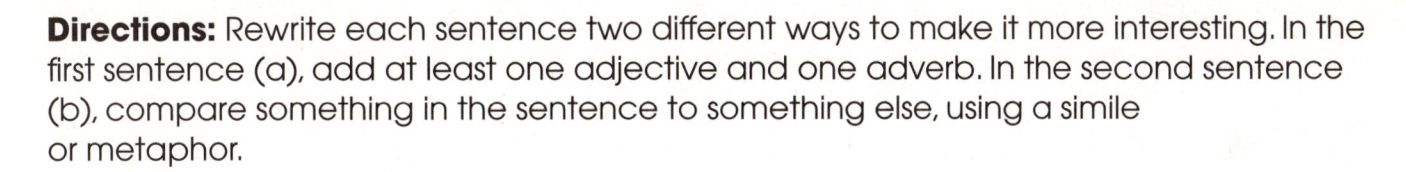

Directions: Rewrite each sentence two different ways to make it more interesting. In the first sentence (a), add at least one adjective and one adverb. In the second sentence (b), compare something in the sentence to something else, using a simile or metaphor.

Example: The baby cried.
　　　　a. The sick baby cried softly all night.
　　　　b. The baby cried louder and louder, like a storm gaining strength.

1. The stranger arrived.

    a. _____

    b. _____

2. The dog barked.

    a. _____

    b. _____

3. The children danced.

    a. _____

    b. _____

4. The moon rose.

    a. _____

    b. _____

Using a Dictionary

Directions: Use the dictionary entry below to answer the questions.

ad-he-sive (ad-he'-siv) *adj.* 1. Tending to adhere; sticky. 2. Gummed so as to adhere. *n.* 3. An adhesive substance such as paste or glue. **ad-he-sive-ly** *adv.* **ad-he-sive-ness** *n.*

1. Based on the first definition of **adhesive**, what do you think **adhere** means?
   _____

2. Which definition of **adhesive** is used in this sentence? The tape was so adhesive that we couldn't peel it loose.
   _____

3. Which part of speech is **adhesive** used as in this sentence? We put a strong adhesive on the package to keep is sealed. _____

4. How many syllables does **adhesive** have? _____

5. Is **adhesive** used as a noun or an adjective in this sentence? The adhesive we chose to use was not very gummy. _____

6. **Adhesive** and variations of the word can be used as what parts of speech?
   _____

Directions: Write sentences using these words.

7. adhesiveness _____
   _____

8. adhesively _____
   _____

9. adhere _____
   _____

Name _____

Online Odyssey

When using the Internet, it is important to be able to tell which sites are reliable and contain accurate information.

Directions: Connie Confused is looking for information about the early frontiersman, Daniel Boone, on the Internet. Help Connie by underlining the Web sites you think might contain relevant and reliable information.

1. the Daniel Boone page of the University of Kentucky Library Web site

2. home page for Daniel Boone High School

3. Danny Loone's own Daniel Boone-themed Web site

4. an article on Daniel Boone from the American Heritage Articles on Frontiersman Web site

5. the home page of the Daniel Boone Coin Club

6. the Daniel Boone page of the Kentucky Historical Society Web site

7. a Web site containing Mrs. Bea Quiet's 5th grade class reports on Daniel Boone

8. the Realsmart family home page containing Timmy Realsmart's research report on Daniel Boone for Mrs. Bea Quiet's 5th grade class

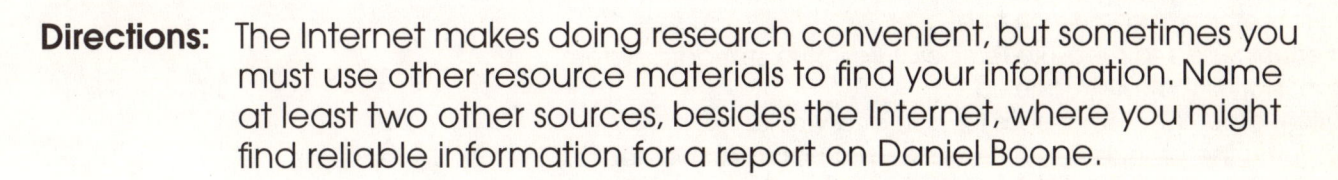

Directions: The Internet makes doing research convenient, but sometimes you must use other resource materials to find your information. Name at least two other sources, besides the Internet, where you might find reliable information for a report on Daniel Boone.

_____
_____
_____

Glossary of Math, Reading, and Language Arts Terms

addition: the operation that combines numbers to create a sum.
adjective: a describing word that tells more about a noun.
adverb: tells when, where, or how about the verb of a sentence.
antonym: words with opposite, or nearly opposite, meanings.
area: the amount of surface in a given boundary, found by multiplying length by width.
articles: any one of the words *a, an,* or *the* used to modify a noun.
autobiography: a written account of your life.
bar graph: displays information by lengths of parallel rectangular bars.
base word (also called root word): the word left after you take off a prefix or a suffix.
Celsius: used to measure temperature in the metric system.
character: a person, animal, or object that a story is about.
climax: the most thrilling part of the story where the problem will or will not be solved.
commutative: a property that allows you to add or multiply two numbers in any order and still get the same answer, such as 2x3=3x2.
composite number: a number that can be divided evenly by numbers other than itself and one.
compound word: a word formed by two or more words.
conclusion: a final decision about something, or the part of a story that tells what happens to the characters.
congruent: figures that are the same shape and the same size.
conjunction: words that join other words, phrases, and sentences.
contraction: shortened forms of two words often using an apostrophe to show where letters are missing.
coordinates: points located on the same graph.
customary measurement: the standard system for measuring, such as cup, pint, quart, gallon, ounce, pound, inch, foot, yard, mile.
decimal: a number with one or more numbers to the right of a decimal point.
decimal point: a dot placed between the ones place and the tenths place of a number.
denominator: the bottom number in a fraction telling the number of parts in the whole.
dialogue: a conversation between two or more people.
diameter: a line segment which passes through the center, joining two points on a circle.
difference: the number received when one number is subtracted from another.
digit: a numeral.
digraph: two consonants pronounced as one sound.
diphthongs: two vowels together that make a new sound.
dividend: a number that is to be divided by another number.
division: shows how many times one number contains another.
divisor: a number by which another number is to be divided.
fact: something known to be true.
Fahrenheit: used to measure temperature in the standard system.
fiction: stories that are made up.
fraction: a number that stands for part of a whole.
geometry: the branch of mathematics that has to do with points, lines, and shapes.
homophone: a word with the same pronunciation as another, but with a different meaning, and often a different spelling, such as *son–sun*.
idiom: a figure of speech or phrase that means something different than what the words actually say, such as "He changed his bad habits and *turned over a new leaf.*"
inference: an educated guess.
integer: any positive or negative whole number, including zero.
mass: the amount or quantity of matter contained in an object.
mean: the average of a set of numbers.
median: the middle number when the numbers are put in order from least to greatest.

metaphor: a direct comparison that does not use *like* or *as*.
metric measurement: a system of measurement based on counting by tens, such as liter, milliliter, gram, kilogram, centimeter, meter, kilometer.
mixed number: a whole number and a fraction together.
mode: the number that occurs most frequently in a set of numbers.
mood: the atmosphere one gets from strong, descriptive language.
multiplication: taking a number and adding to itself a certain number of times.
nonfiction: stories that are true.
noun: a word that names a person, place, or thing.
numerator: the top number in a fraction showing the number of parts out of the whole.
operations: addition, subtraction, multiplication, division.
opinion: a belief based on what a person thinks instead of what is known to be true.
ordered pair: lists the horizontal and the vertical location of the point, such as (3,4).
parallel lines: two lines that never intersect.
perimeter: the distance around an object found by adding the lengths and widths.
perpendicular: two lines that intersect at a ninety degree angle.
place value: shown by where the numeral is in the number.
plot: explains the events in a story that create a problem.
plural: a form of a word that names or refers to more than one person or thing.
point of view: the attitude a person has about a particular topic.
polygon: a closed figure that has three or more sides.
prefix: a part that is added to the beginning of a word that changes the word's meaning.
preposition: a word that comes before a noun or pronoun, showing the relationship of that noun or pronoun to another word in the sentence.
prime number: any number greater than one that can be divided evenly by itself and the number one.
probability: the likelihood or chance that something will happen.
product: the number received when two numbers are multiplied together.
pronoun: a word that is used in place of a noun.
proofreading: reading to find and correct errors.
punctuation: the marks that qualify sentences, such as a period, comma, question mark, exclamation point, and apostrophe.
quotient: the number received when a number is divided.
radius: a line segment from the center of the circle to any point on the circle.
reading strategies: main idea, supporting details, context clues, fact/opinion.
regrouping: borrowing numbers from another column to complete the operation.
remainder: the number left over when a number cannot be divided evenly.
resolution: tells how the characters solve the story problem.
rounding: expressing a number to the nearest ten, hundred, thousand, and so on.
setting: the place and time that a story happens.
simile: a comparison using *like* or *as*.
subtraction: "taking away" one number from another to find the difference.
suffix: a part added to the end of a word to change the word's meaning.
sum: the number received when two numbers are added together.
symmetry: when both sides of an object are exactly the same.
synonym: words that mean the same, or almost the same, thing.
theme: a message or central idea of the story.
variable: a letter used to represent a number value in an expression or an equation.
verb: a word that can show action.
verb tense: tells whether the action is happening in the past, present, or future.
volume: the measurement of capacity found by multiplying the length, width, and height of the object.
whole numbers: a set of numbers that includes zero and all the counting numbers, such as 0, 1, 2, 3 . . .

Summer Success — Answer Key

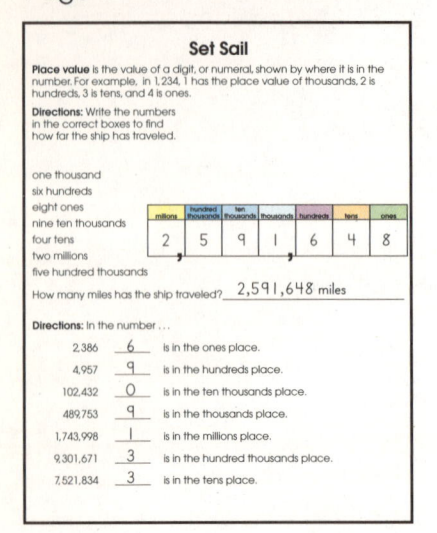

Page 5 — Set Sail

Place value is the value of a digit, or numeral, shown by where it is in the number. For example, in 1,234, 1 has the place value of thousands, 2 is hundreds, 3 is tens, and 4 is ones.

Directions: Write the numbers in the correct boxes to find how far the ship has traveled.

- one thousand
- six hundreds
- eight ones
- nine ten thousands
- four tens
- two millions
- five hundred thousands

millions	hundred thousands	ten thousands	thousands	hundreds	tens	ones
2	5	9	1	6	4	8

How many miles has the ship traveled? **2,591,648 miles**

Directions: In the number …

- 2,386 — **6** is in the ones place.
- 4,957 — **9** is in the hundreds place.
- 102,432 — **0** is in the ten thousands place.
- 489,753 — **9** is in the thousands place.
- 1,743,998 — **1** is in the millions place.
- 9,301,671 — **3** is in the hundred thousands place.
- 7,521,834 — **3** is in the tens place.

Page 6 — Rounding and Estimating

Rounding numbers and **estimating** answers is an easy way of finding the approximate answer without writing out the problem or using a calculator.

Directions: Fill in the bubble next to the correct answer.

Round to the nearest **ten**:
1. 73 — ● 70
2. 48 — ● 50
3. 65 — ● 70
4. 85 — ● 90
5. (blank) — ● 90
6. 37 — ● 40

Round to the nearest **hundred**:
7. 139 — ● 100
8. 782 — ● 800
9. 390 — ● 400
10. 640 — ● 600
11. 525 — ● 500
12. 457 — ● 500

Round to the nearest **thousand**:
13. 1,375 — ● 1,000
14. 21,800 — ● 22,000

15. Sam wanted to buy a new computer. He knew he only had about $1,200 to spend. Which of the following ones could he afford to buy? **$1,165**

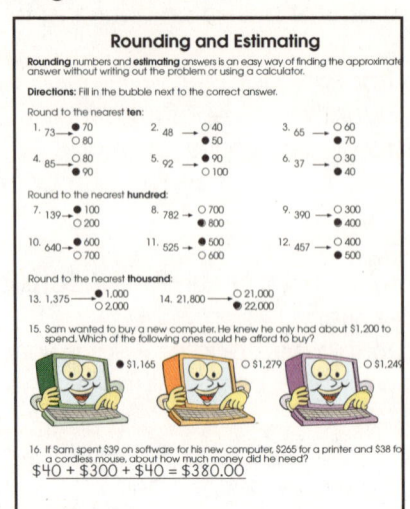

16. If Sam spent $39 on software for his new computer, $265 for a printer and $38 for a cordless mouse, about how much money did he need?
$40 + $300 + $40 = **$380.00**

Page 7 — What Do You Think?

Estimate the answer to each question. Use a timer, watch, or clock that measures seconds to time the activity. Then, record the actual answer. How close was the estimate?

Most answers will vary.

1. How many jumping jacks can you do in 15 seconds?
2. How many seconds does it take to say the alphabet backwards?
3. How many light bulbs are there in your home?
4. How many seconds does it take to tie both shoes?
5. How many times does the letter "p" appear on this page?
6. How many spoonfuls of water does it take to fill a small drinking glass?
7. How high can you count aloud in 15 seconds?
8. How many steps does it take to walk around the edge of the largest room in your home?
9. How many numbers between 1 and 99 have the numeral 2 in them?
10. How many seconds does it take to sing "Happy Birthday to You"?

Page 8 — Field Day

Podium: 1st = 24, 2nd = 26, 3rd = 27

The winners of the 800-meter relay want to know their winning times. Help them fill in their scores. First, find the mean, mode, and median for each list of numbers. Then, follow the directions below. Remember, the **mean** is the average of the numbers, the **median** is the middle number when the group is put in order, and the **mode** is the number that appears most frequently.

numbers	mean	median	mode
24, 20, 21, 29, 24, 26	24	24	24
24, 26, 22, 26, 28, 30	26	26	26
23, 26, 19, 27, 27, 28, 18	24	26	27

The winning team had a time in seconds equal to the mean of the first problem. The second-place team had a time equal to the median of the second problem. The third-place team had a time equal to the mode of the third problem. Write the times on the cards.

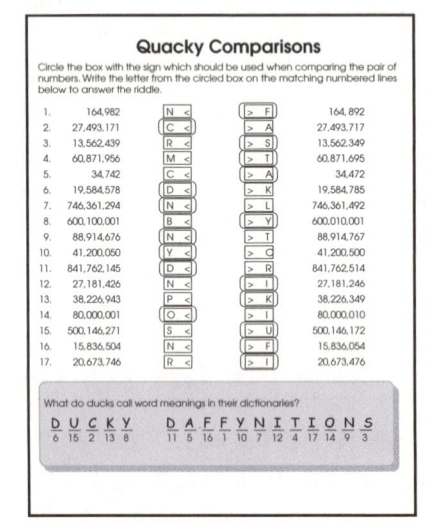

Page 9 — Quacky Comparisons

Circle the box with the sign which should be used when comparing the pair of numbers. Write the letter from the circled box on the matching numbered lines below to answer the riddle.

1. 164,982 **N <** 164,892
2. 27,493,171 **C <** 27,493,717
3. 13,562,439 **R >** 13,562,349
4. 60,871,956 **M >** 60,871,695
5. 34,742 **C <** 34,472 *(actually: 34,742 > 34,472)*
6. 19,584,578 **D <** 19,584,785
7. 746,361,294 **N <** 746,361,492
8. 600,100,001 **M <** 600,010,001 *(>)*
9. 88,914,676 **N <** 88,914,767
10. 41,200,050 **Y <** 41,200,500
11. 841,762,145 **D <** 841,762,514
12. 27,181,426 **A <** 27,181,246 *(>)*
13. 38,226,943 **P <** 38,226,349 *(>)*
14. 80,000,001 **O <** 80,000,010
15. 500,146,271 **S >** 500,146,172
16. 15,836,504 **N <** 15,836,054 *(>)*
17. 20,673,746 **R <** 20,673,476 *(>)*

What do ducks call word meanings in their dictionaries?

D U C K Y   D A F F Y N I T I O N S
6 15 2 13 8   11 15 16 1 10 7 12 4 17 14 9 3

Page 10 — Deep Blue Sea

An **integer** is any positive or negative whole number, or zero. Negative integers are numbers less than zero. The opposite of any number is found the same distance from 0 on a number line.

Example: 35 below zero can be written as –35. The opposite of 6 is –6. The opposite of –41 is 41. The opposite of 0 is 0.

Write a number for each description.
1. 5 feet below sea level — **–5**
2. 14 degrees below zero — **–14**
3. a loss of $10 — **–10**
4. climbing down 9 feet into a cave — **–9**
5. a 2 yard gain in a football game — **+2**
6. 3 fewer fish than the day before — **–3**
7. no change — **0**
8. driving a car 11 feet in reverse — **–11**

Write a description for each integer.
- –6 **feet below ground**
- –14 **feet below sea level**
- –3 **3 degrees below zero**
- –7 **degrees colder than last night**
- 0 **no change**
- 8 **degrees above zero**
- 4 **foot high tree**
- –4 **eggs less collected today**

Write the opposite number.
- 6 — **–6**   0 — **same**
- 4 — **–4**   –14 — **14**
- –9 — **9**   –7 — **7**
- 5 — **–5**   25 — **–25**

Page 11 — Pattern Puzzles

Figuring out the secret to a number pattern or code can send you into "thinking overtime."

Directions: Discover the pattern for each set of numbers. Then write the missing numbers.

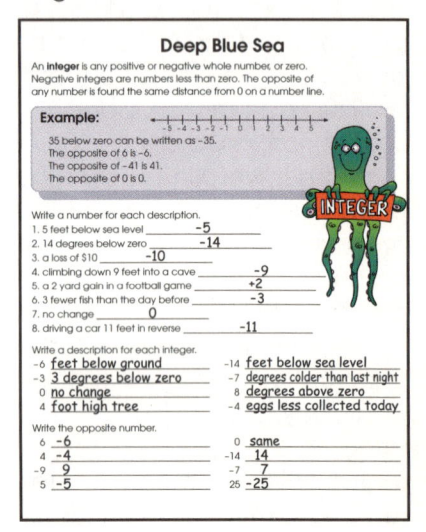

a) 20, 21, 19, 20, **18**, 19, 17, **16**, **14**, 15, **13**, 14
b) 1, 6, 16, 31, 51, **76**, **106**, 141, **181**, 226.
c) 3, 5, 9, 15, **23**, **33**, 45, **59**, 75.
d) 55, 52, 50, 49, 46, **44**, **43**, **40**, 38, 37, **35**.
e) 1, 3, 6, 10, 15, 21, **28**, **36**, **45**, 55, 66, 78.
f) 10, 16, 13, 19, 16, **22**, 19, **25**, 22, **28**, 25.
g) 3, 4, 7, 12, **19**, **28**, 39, 52, **67**, **84**.
h) 100, 90, 95, 85, 90, 80, 85, **75**, **80**, **70**, 75.

Directions: Make up a number pattern of your own. Have a parent, brother or sister figure it out! — **Answers will vary.**

Directions: Follow the instructions to solve the number puzzler. Use only these numbers: 2, 4, 5, 7, 8, 11, 13, 14, 16. Each number may only be used once. Write even numbers in the squares. Write odd numbers in the circles. Each row must add up to 26. *Hint: Work the puzzle in pencil, so you can erase and retry numbers if needed.*

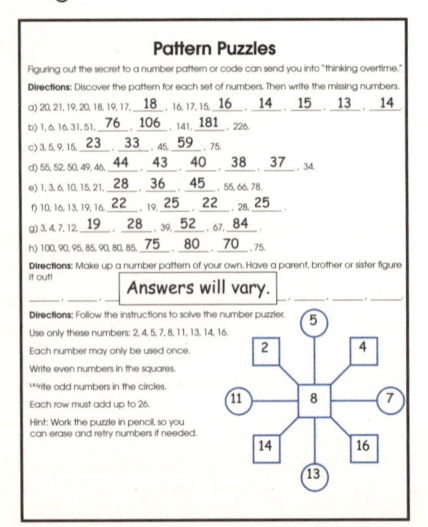

Cross diagram with center 8:
- Top: 5, 2, 4
- Left: 11, 8, 7
- Right: (7), (middle), (16)
- Bottom: 14, 16
(Numbers shown: 5, 2, 4, 11, 8, 7, 14, 16, 13)

Page 12 — Going in Circles

Directions: Where the circles meet, write the sum of the numbers from the circles to the right and left and above and below. The first row shows you what to do.

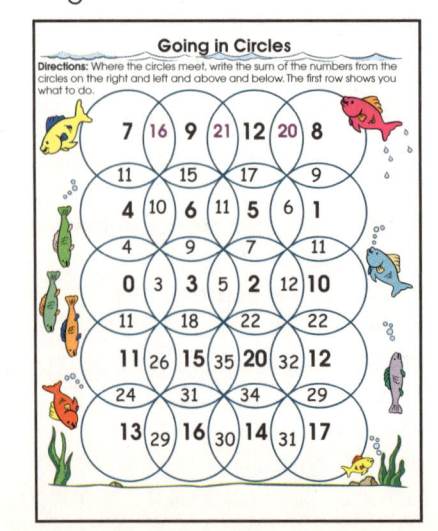

Row 1: 7 **16** 9 **21** 12 **20** 8
Row 2: **11** **15** **9** **11**
Row 3: 4 **10** 6 **11** 5 **6** 1
Row 4: **9** **7** **6** **11**
Row 5: 0 **3** 2 **5** 3 **12** 10
Row 6: **11** **8** **12** **22**
Row 7: 11 **26** 15 **35** 20 **32** 12
Row 8: **24** **31** **24** **29**
Row 9: 13 **29** 16 **30** 14 **31** 17

Page 13 — Bringing Fido Home

Regrouping uses 10 ones to form one 10, 10 tens to form one hundred, one 10 and 5 ones to form 15, and so on.

Directions: Add using regrouping. Color in all the boxes with a 5 in the answer to help the dog find its way home.

63 + 22 = **85**	5,268 + 4,910 + 1,683 = **11,861**	248 + 463 = **711**	291 + 543 = **834**	2,934 + 112 = **3,046**
1,736 + 5,367 = **7,103**	2,946 + 7,384 = **10,330**	3,245 + 1,239 + 981 = **5,465**	738 + 692 = **1,430**	896 + 728 = **1,624**	594 + 738 = **1,332**
2,603 + 5,004 = **7,607**	4,507 + 289 = **4,796**	1,483 + 6,753 = **8,236**	1,258 + 6,301 = **7,559**	27 + 469 + 6,002 = **6,498**	4,637 + 7,531 = **12,168**
782 + 65 = **847**	485 + 276 = **761**	3,421 + 8,064 = **11,485**		
48 + 93 + 26 = **167**	90 + 263 + 864 = **1,217**	362 + 453 + 800 = **1,615**		

86

SUMMER SUCCESS

Page 14: Snack Subtract
Directions: Subtract using regrouping.

Page 15: Stocking Sue's Pond
Directions: Add or subtract, using regrouping when needed.

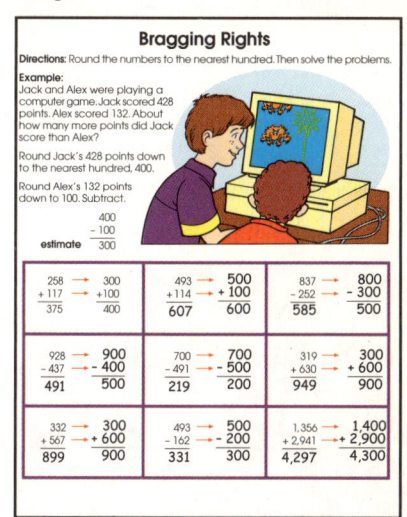

Sue stocked her pond with 263 bass and 187 trout. 97 fish swam away in a flood. How many fish are left? **353 fish**

Page 16: Bragging Rights
Directions: Round the numbers to the nearest hundred. Then solve the problems.

Page 17: Lots of Fish in the Sea
When multiplying a number by 10, the answer is the number with a 0. It is like counting by tens.
When multiplying a number by 100, the answer is the number with two 0's. When multiplying by 1,000, the answer is the number with three 0's.

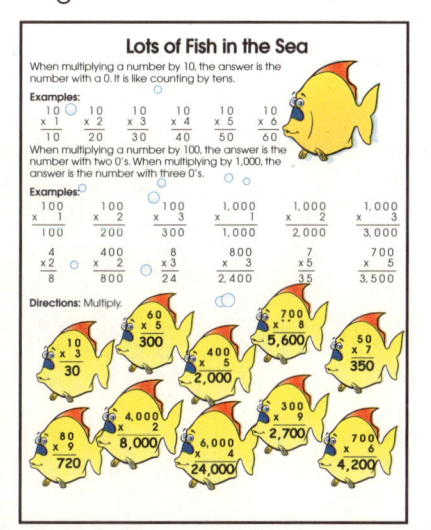

Page 18: Birds of a Feather
Directions: Multiply.

Page 19: A Worm Divided
Division is a way to find out how many times one number is contained in another number. For example, 28 ÷ 7 = 4 means that there are 4 groups of 7 in 28.

Division problems can be written two ways: 36 ÷ 6 = 6 or 6)36

These are the parts of a division problem:
dividend → 36 ÷ 6 = 6 ← quotient / divisor
divisor → 6)36 ← dividend

Directions: Divide.

Page 20: Farming for Answers
Directions: Divide. Then check each answer on another sheet of paper by multiplying it by the divisor and adding the remainder.

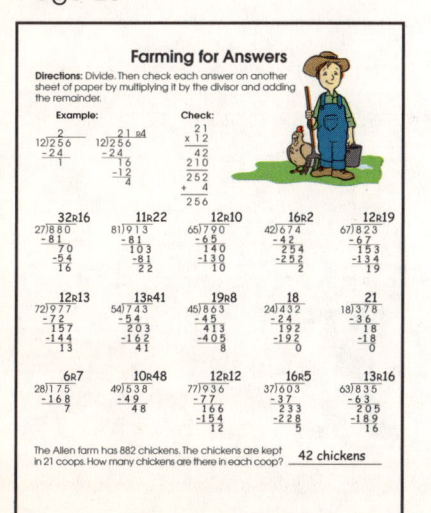

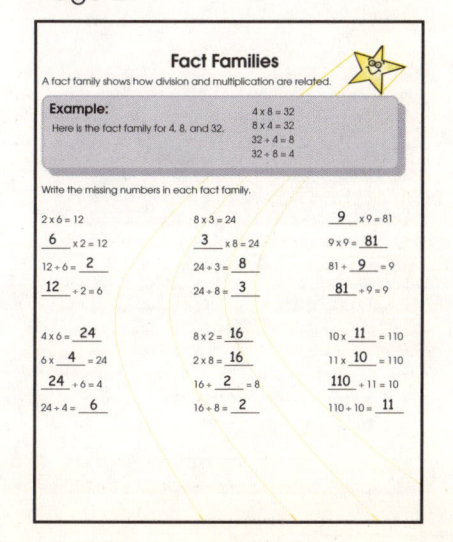

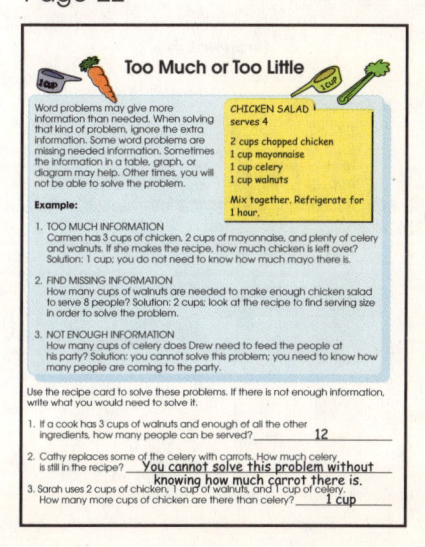

The Allen farm has 882 chickens. The chickens are kept in 21 coops. How many chickens are there in each coop? **42 chickens**

Page 21: Fact Families
A fact family shows how division and multiplication are related.

Example: Here is the fact family for 4, 8, and 32.
4 × 8 = 32
8 × 4 = 32
32 ÷ 4 = 8
32 ÷ 8 = 4

Write the missing numbers in each fact family.

Page 22: Too Much or Too Little
Word problems may give more information than needed. When solving that kind of problem, ignore the extra information. Some word problems are missing needed information. Sometimes the information in a table, graph, or diagram may help. Other times, you will not be able to solve the problem.

CHICKEN SALAD serves 4
2 cups chopped chicken
1 cup mayonnaise
1 cup celery
1 cup walnuts
Mix together. Refrigerate for 1 hour.

Example:
1. TOO MUCH INFORMATION
Carmen has 3 cups of chicken, 2 cups of mayonnaise, and plenty of celery and walnuts. If she makes the recipe, how much chicken is left over?
Solution: 1 cup; you do not need to know how much mayo there is.

2. FIND MISSING INFORMATION
How many cups of walnuts are needed to make enough chicken salad to serve 8 people? Solution: 2 cups; look at the recipe to find serving size in order to solve the problem.

3. NOT ENOUGH INFORMATION
How many cups of celery does Drew need to feed the people at his party? Solution: you cannot solve this problem; you need to know how many people are coming to the party.

Use the recipe card to solve these problems. If there is not enough information, write what you would need to solve it.

1. If a cook has 3 cups of walnuts and enough of all the other ingredients, how many people can be served? **12**

2. Cathy replaces some of the celery with carrots. How much celery is still in the recipe? **You cannot solve this problem without knowing how much carrot there is.**

3. Sarah uses 2 cups of chicken, 1 cup of walnuts, and 1 cup of celery. How many more cups of chicken are there than celery? **1 cup**

SUMMER SUCCESS

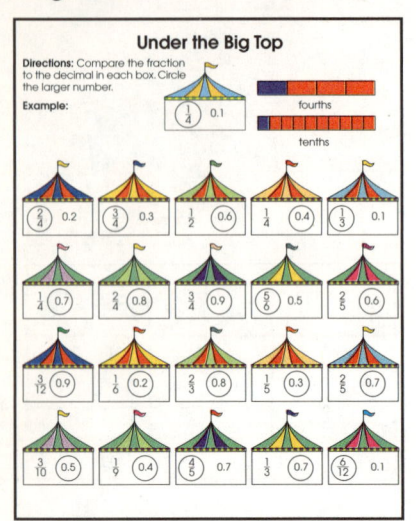

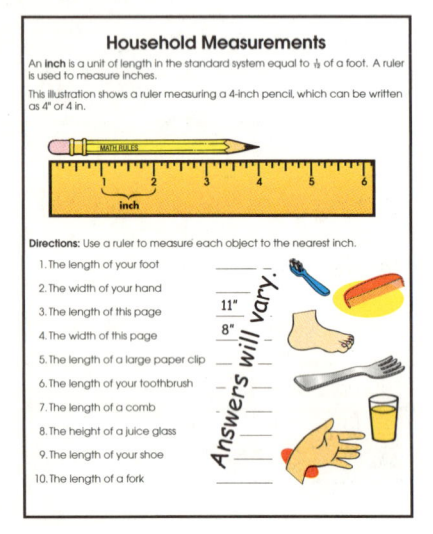

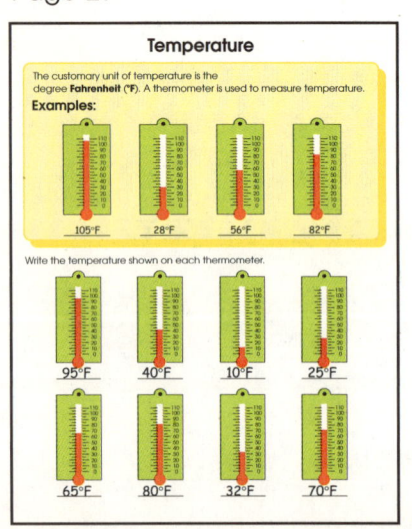

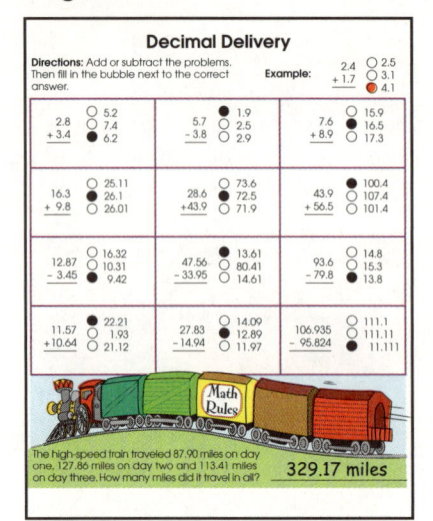

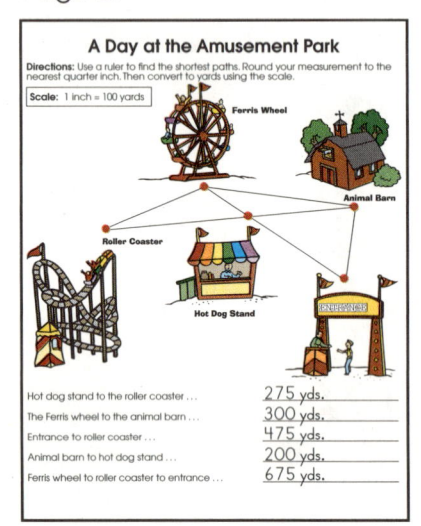

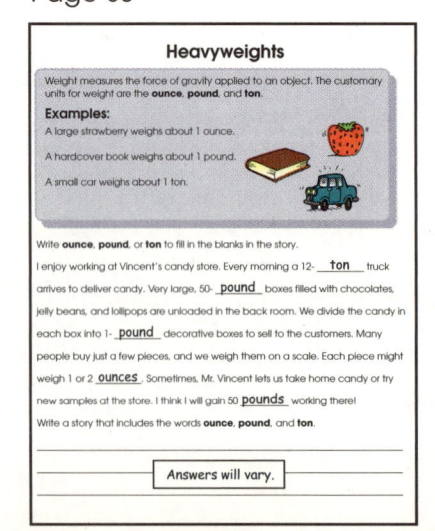

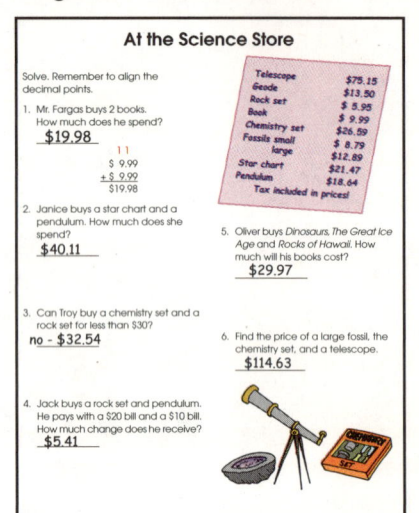

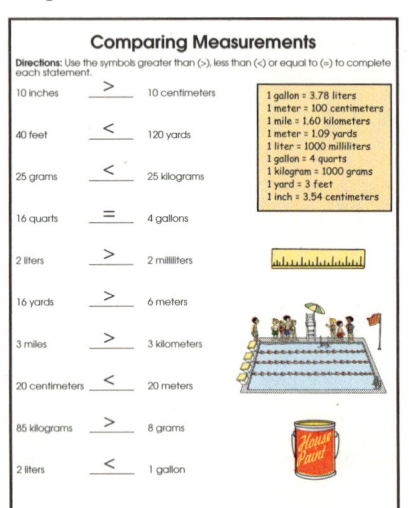

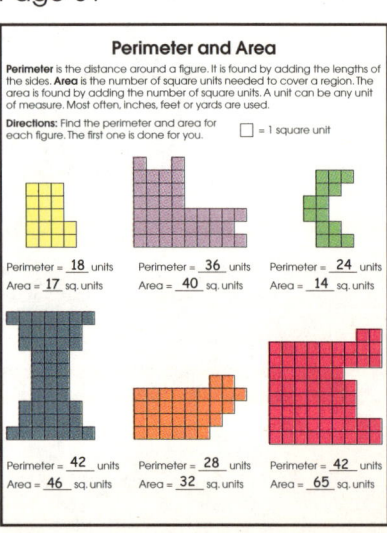

Page 23 — Under the Big Top
Answer key for fraction/decimal comparison:
- 2/4 ○0.2 1/3 ●0.3 1/2 ●0.6 1/4 ●0.1 1/3 ●0.1
- 1/4 ●0.7 2/4 ●0.8 3/4 ○0.5 2/5 ○0.6
- 3/12 ●0.9 1/6 ○0 2/3 ●0.8 1/5 ●0.3 4/6 ●0.7
- 3/10 ●0.5 1/9 ●0.4 2/4 ●0.6 1/6 ○0.7 6/12 ●0.1

Page 24 — Decimal Delivery
Example: 2.4 + 1.7 = ●4.1

- 2.8 + 3.4 = ●6.2
- 5.7 − 3.8 = ●1.9
- 7.6 + 8.9 = ●16.5
- 16.3 + 9.8 = ●26.01
- 28.6 + 43.9 = ●72.5
- 43.9 + 56.5 = ●100.4
- 12.87 − 3.45 = ●9.42
- 47.56 − 33.95 = ●13.61
- 93.6 − 79.8 = ●13.8
- 11.57 + 10.64 = ●22.21
- 27.83 − 14.94 = ●12.89
- 106.935 − 95.824 = ●11.111

The high-speed train traveled 87.90 miles on day one, 127.86 miles on day two and 113.41 miles on day three. How many miles did it travel in all? **329.17 miles**

Page 25 — At the Science Store
1. Mr. Fargas buys 2 books. How much does he spend? **$19.98**
2. Janice buys a star chart and a pendulum. How much does she spend? **$40.11**
3. Can Troy buy a chemistry set and a rock set for less than $30? **no − $32.54**
4. Jack buys a rock set and pendulum. He pays with a $20 bill and a $10 bill. How much change does he receive? **$5.41**
5. Oliver buys Dinosaurs, The Great Ice Age and Rocks of Hawaii. How much will his books cost? **$29.97**
6. Find the price of a large fossil, the chemistry set, and a telescope. **$114.63**

Page 26 — Household Measurements
Answers will vary.

Page 27 — A Day at the Amusement Park
- Hot dog stand to the roller coaster … **275 yds.**
- The Ferris wheel to the animal barn … **300 yds.**
- Entrance to roller coaster … **475 yds.**
- Animal barn to hot dog stand … **200 yds.**
- Ferris wheel to roller coaster to entrance … **675 yds.**

Page 28 — Comparing Measurements
- 10 inches **>** 10 centimeters
- 40 feet **<** 120 yards
- 25 grams **<** 25 kilograms
- 16 quarts **=** 4 gallons
- 2 liters **>** 2 milliliters
- 16 yards **>** 6 meters
- 3 miles **>** 3 kilometers
- 20 centimeters **<** 20 meters
- 85 kilograms **>** 8 grams
- 2 liters **<** 1 gallon

Page 29 — Temperature
Examples: 105°F, 28°F, 56°F, 82°F
- 95°F, 40°F, 10°F, 25°F
- 65°F, 80°F, 32°F, 70°F

Page 30 — Heavyweights
I enjoy working at Vincent's candy store. Every morning a 12-**ton** truck arrives to deliver candy. Very large, 50-**pound** boxes filled with chocolates, jelly beans, and lollipops are unloaded in the back room. We divide the candy in each box into 1-**pound** decorative boxes to sell to the customers. Many people buy just a few pieces, and we weigh them on a scale. Each piece might weigh 1 or 2 **ounces**. Sometimes, Mr. Vincent lets us take home candy or try new samples at the store. I think I will gain 50 **pounds** working there!

Write a story: **Answers will vary.**

Page 31 — Perimeter and Area
- Perimeter = **18** units, Area = **17** sq. units
- Perimeter = **36** units, Area = **40** sq. units
- Perimeter = **24** units, Area = **14** sq. units
- Perimeter = **42** units, Area = **46** sq. units
- Perimeter = **28** units, Area = **32** sq. units
- Perimeter = **42** units, Area = **65** sq. units

SUMMER SUCCESS

Page 32
How Much Does It Hold?

Volume is the measurement of capacity. The formula for finding the volume of a box is length times width times height (L x W x H). The answer is given in cubic units.

Directions: Solve the problems.

Example:
Height 8 ft.
Length 8 ft.
Width 8 ft. L x W x H = volume
8' x 8' x 8' = 512 cubic ft. or 512 ft.³

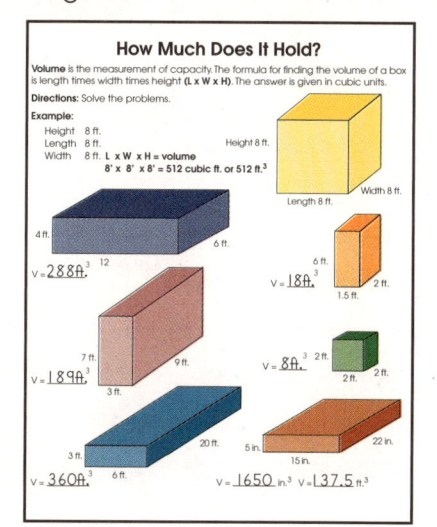

V = 288 ft.³
V = 18 ft.³
V = 8 ft.³
V = 189 ft.³
V = 360 ft.³
V = 1650 in.³
V = 37.5 ft.³

Page 33
Lines

Examples:
- point A
- line segment CD (has 2 endpoints)
- line ZM (extends forever in both directions)
- ray LP (extends in one direction forever)
- vertical line segment WX
- horizontal line segment YZ
- parallel lines KL, PQ
- perpendicular rays GF, GH

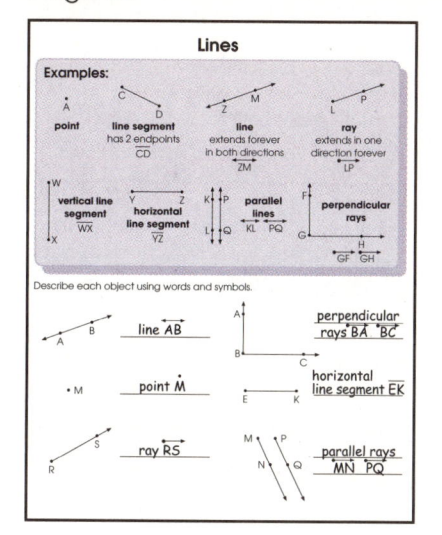

Describe each object using words and symbols.
- line AB
- point M
- ray RS
- perpendicular rays BA, BC
- horizontal line segment EK
- parallel rays MN, PQ

Page 34
Angles

The point at which two line segments meet is called an **angle**. There are three types of angles — right, acute and obtuse.

- A **right angle** is formed when the two lines meet at 90°.
- An **acute angle** is formed when the two lines meet at less than 90°.
- An **obtuse angle** is formed when the two lines meet at greater than 90°.

Angles can be measured with a protractor or index card. With a protractor, align the bottom edge of the angle with the bottom of the protractor, with the angle point at the circle of the protractor. Note the direction of the other ray and the number of degrees of the angle.

- right
- acute
- obtuse

Place the corner of an index card in the corner of the angle. If the edges line up with the card, it is a right angle. If not, the angle is acute or obtuse.

- right
- acute
- obtuse

Directions: Use a protractor or index card to identify the following angles as right, obtuse or acute.

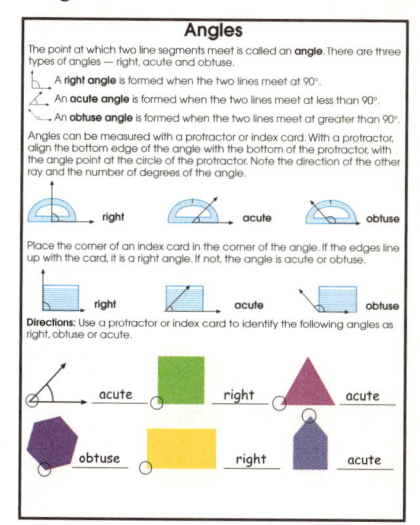

- acute
- right
- acute
- obtuse
- right
- acute

Page 35
Angles

When two line segments come together, they form an angle.
- angle BAC
- ∠ BAC
- ∠ A
- sides
- vertex

Angles are measured in units called degrees (°). A half-circle has 180°. Angles can be measured with a protractor.

The number of degrees in an angle determines what kind of angle it is.

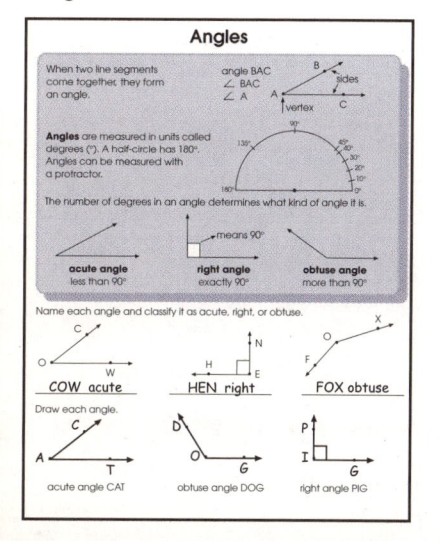

- means 90°
- acute angle (less than 90°)
- right angle (exactly 90°)
- obtuse angle (more than 90°)

Name each angle and classify it as acute, right, or obtuse.
- COW acute
- HEN right
- FOX obtuse

Draw each angle.
- acute angle CAT
- obtuse angle DOG
- right angle PIG

Page 36
Triangle Groups

Triangles can also be classified by the kinds of angles they have.
- acute (all three angles less than 90°)
- right (one angle is exactly 90°)
- obtuse (one angle is more than 90°)

An **isosceles** triangle is a triangle with at least two equal sides.

Draw each triangle.
- acute triangle
- right triangle
- obtuse triangle
- obtuse isosceles triangle

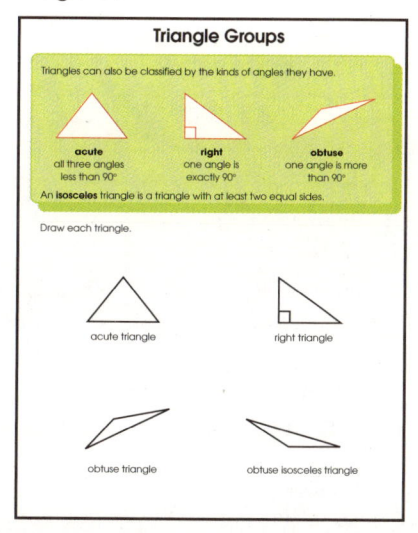

Page 37
Circles

A **circle** is a round figure. It is named by its center. A **radius** is a line segment from the center of a circle to any point on the circle. A **diameter** is a line segment with both end points on the circle. The diameter always passes through the center of the circle.

Directions: Name the radius, diameter and circle.

Example:
- Circle A
- Radius AB
- Diameter DC

- Circle X
- Radius XY
- Diameter WZ

- Circle B
- Radius AB
- Diameter CD

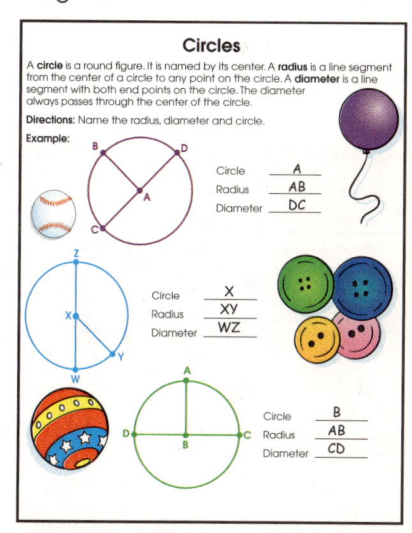

Page 38
Polygons

A **polygon** is a closed figure with three or more sides.

Examples:
- triangle (3 sides)
- square (4 equal sides)
- rectangle (4 sides)
- pentagon (5 sides)
- hexagon (6 sides)
- octagon (8 sides)

Directions: Identify the polygons.
- octagon
- rectangle
- square
- hexagon
- pentagon
- triangle

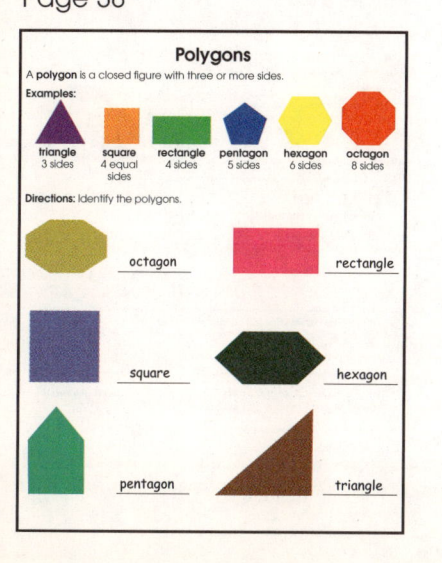

Page 39
Similar, Congruent, and Symmetrical Figures

Similar figures have the same shape but have varying sizes.

Figures that are **congruent** have identical shapes but different orientations. That means they face in different directions.

Symmetrical figures can be divided equally into two identical parts.

Directions: Cross out the shape that does not belong in each group. Label the two remaining shapes as similar, congruent or symmetrical.

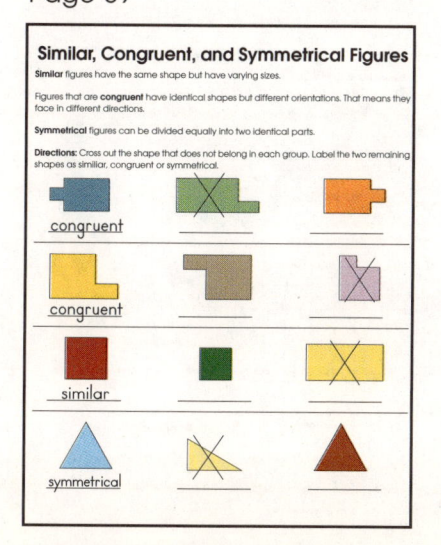

- congruent
- congruent
- similar
- symmetrical

Page 40
What's Next?

Draw the next three shapes in the pattern.

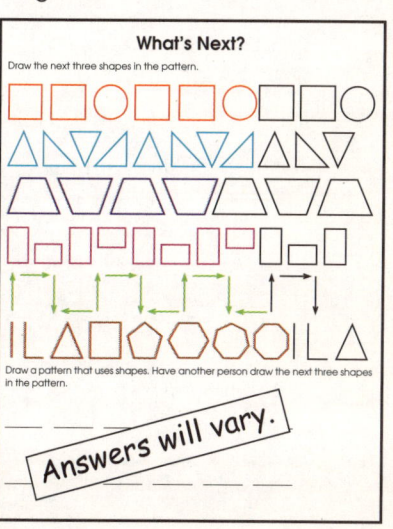

Draw a pattern that uses shapes. Have another person draw the next three shapes in the pattern.

Answers will vary.

89

Summer Success

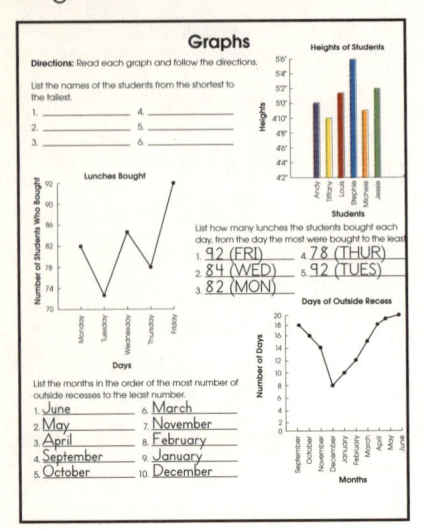

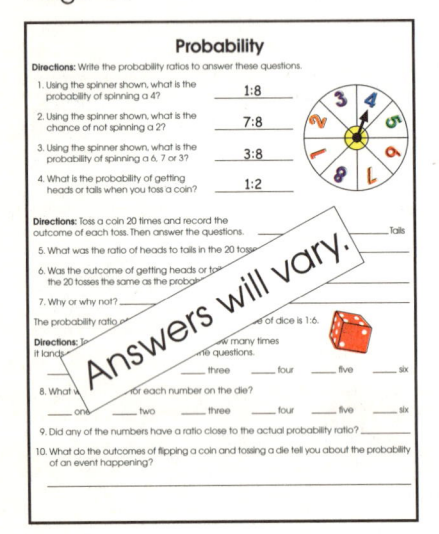

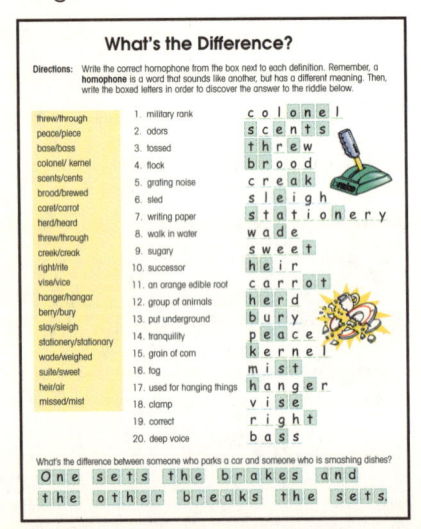

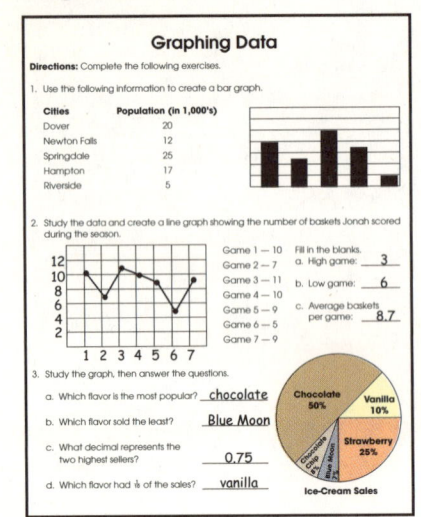

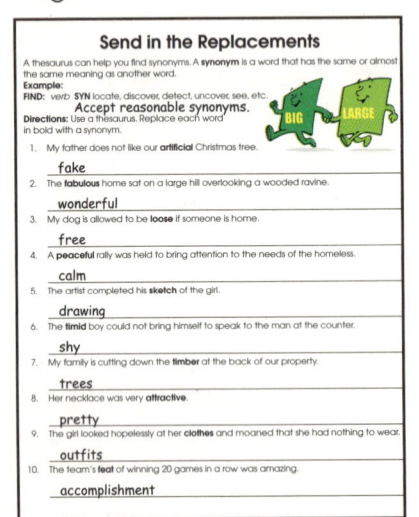

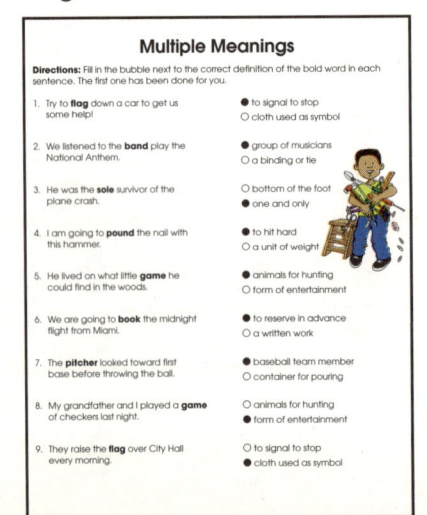

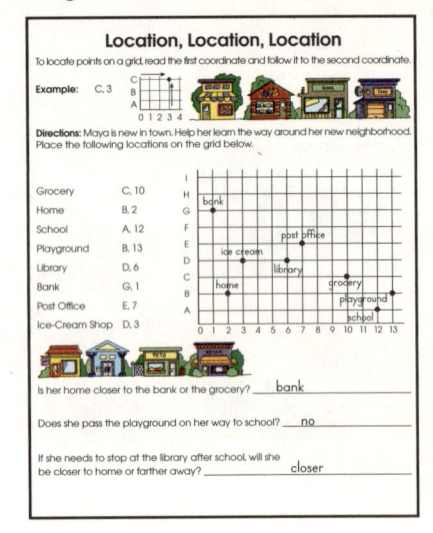

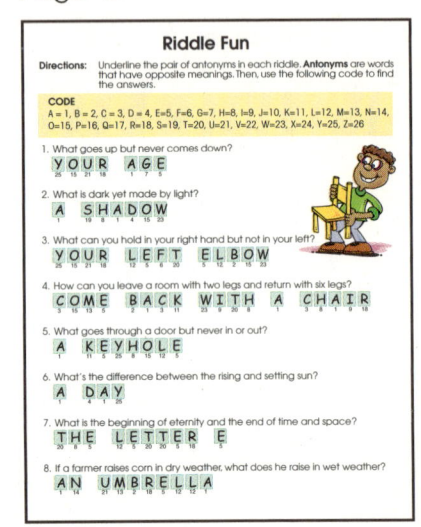

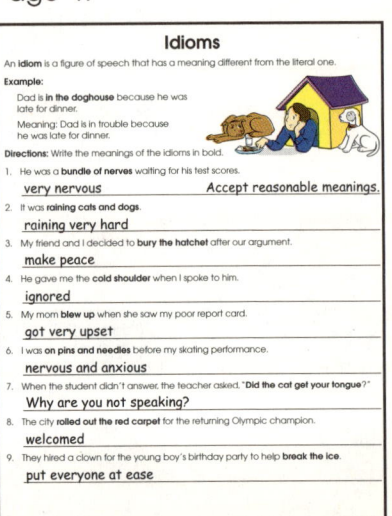

Page 41 — Graphs
List the names of the students from the shortest to the tallest.
(answers not fully visible)

List how many lunches the students bought each day, from the day the most were bought to the least.
1. 92 (FRI)   4. 78 (THUR)
2. 84 (WED)   5. 92 (TUES)
3. 82 (MON)

List the months in the order of the most number of outside recesses to the least number.
1. June   6. March
2. May   7. November
3. April   8. February
4. September   9. January
5. October   10. December

Page 42 — Graphing Data
Fill in the blanks:
a. High game: 3
b. Low game: 6
c. Average baskets per game: 8.7

a. Which flavor is the most popular? chocolate
b. Which flavor sold the least? Blue Moon
c. What decimal represents the two highest sellers? 0.75
d. Which flavor had ⅛ of the sales? vanilla

Page 43 — Location, Location, Location
Is her home closer to the bank or the grocery? bank
Does she pass the playground on her way to school? no
If she needs to stop at the library after school, will she be closer to home or farther away? closer

Page 44 — Probability
1. 1:8
2. 7:8
3. 3:8
4. 1:2

Answers will vary.

Page 45 — Send in the Replacements
1. fake
2. wonderful
3. free
4. calm
5. drawing
6. shy
7. trees
8. pretty
9. outfits
10. accomplishment

Page 46 — Riddle Fun
1. YOUR AGE
2. A SHADOW
3. YOUR LEFT ELBOW
4. COME BACK WITH A CHAIR
5. A KEYHOLE
6. A DAY
7. THE LETTER E
8. AN UMBRELLA

Page 47 — What's the Difference?
1. colonel
2. scents
3. threw
4. brood
5. creak
6. sleigh
7. stationery
8. wade
9. sweet
10. heir
11. carrot
12. herd
13. bury
14. peace
15. kernel
16. mist
17. hanger
18. vise
19. right
20. bass

Riddle answer: One sets the brakes and the other breaks the sets.

Page 48 — Multiple Meanings
1. to signal to stop
2. group of musicians
3. one and only
4. to hit hard
5. animals for hunting
6. to reserve in advance
7. baseball team member
8. form of entertainment
9. cloth used as symbol

Page 49 — Idioms
1. very nervous
2. raining very hard
3. make peace
4. ignored
5. got very upset
6. nervous and anxious
7. Why are you not speaking?
8. welcomed
9. put everyone at ease

Accept reasonable meanings.

SUMMER SUCCESS

Page 50 — Pick the Prefix

A **prefix** is a group of letters added to the beginning of a word. When a prefix is added, the meaning of the word is changed. Here are some prefixes and their meanings.

Prefix	Meaning
un	not, opposite of
re	again, back
in	not
dis	not, lack of

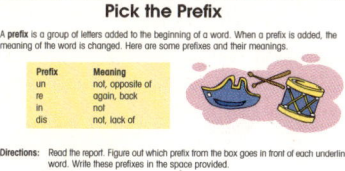

Directions: Read the report. Figure out which prefix from the box goes in front of each underlined word. Write these prefixes in the space provided.

During the American Revolution, many soldiers were **un**happy. Some had never been away from home before, and they were **dis**satisfied with how they had to live. But the cause was important to them, so they tried not to be **dis**couraged.

The Battle of Bunker Hill was the first great battle of the American Revolution. The American Army had to **re**treat. The soldiers may have lost the battle, but the difference between the number of soldiers on each side was greatly **un**fair. In addition, the British army had better weapons and what seemed like **in**destructible powers. However, now the American Patriots were determined and **un**stoppable. During battles, their aim may

have sometimes been **in**accurate. Nevertheless, they began to **re**gain their strength.

Eventually, under the leadership of General George Washington, the American army overcame its **dis**advantage and won the war. Had it not been for the bravery of these largely **un**trained soldiers, the United States may never have been born.

Page 51 — Find the Suffix

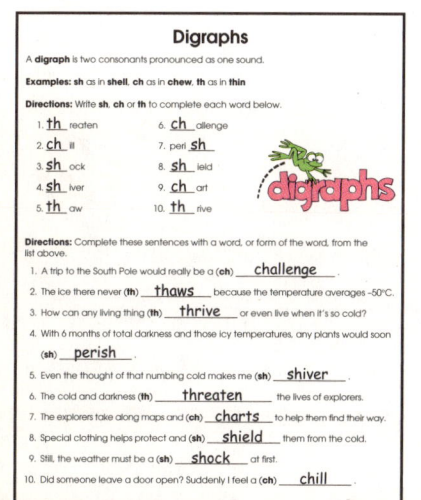

Suffixes are word parts added to the endings of words. When you add a suffix to a word, its meaning as well as its part of speech is changed. Also, sometimes the spelling changes.

Directions: Read each sentence. Change each underlined word by adding the suffix **ful**, **ible**, or **ly**. Write the new word on the line.

1. Mark and his dog headed toward the cave quick. — quickly
2. The play dog ran ahead. — playful
3. As they neared the entrance, the boy was hope about what they would find. — hopeful
4. The dog eager waited while the boy looked over the area. — eagerly
5. Mark knew the sense thing was to turn around. — sensible
6. He wondered if their walk through the cave would go smooth. — smoothly
7. He hoped nothing horror would happen. — horrible
8. They would have to be flex enough to get around all the curves. — flexible
9. Sudden, there was a loud noise. — Suddenly
10. Mark and his dog jumped when they heard the noise and ran rapid toward home. — rapidly

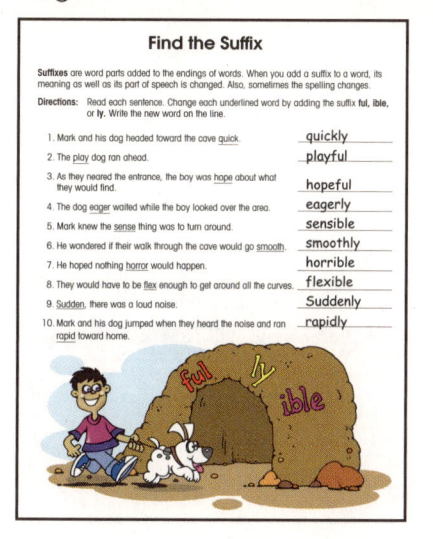

Page 52 — Hunt for Roots

Directions: The words in the box have Latin and Greek roots. Find the words from the box in the puzzle. Look across, down, backward, and diagonally. Circle the words.

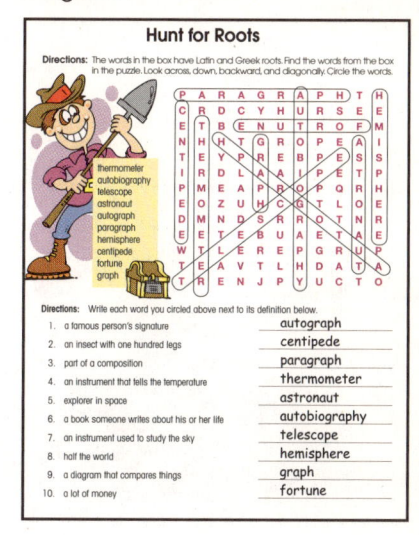

thermometer, autobiography, telescope, astronaut, autograph, paragraph, hemisphere, centipede, fortune, graph

Directions: Write each word you circled above next to its definition below.

1. a famous person's signature — autograph
2. an insect with one hundred legs — centipede
3. part of a composition — paragraph
4. an instrument that tells the temperature — thermometer
5. explorer in space — astronaut
6. a book someone writes about his or her life — autobiography
7. an instrument used to study the sky — telescope
8. half the world — hemisphere
9. a diagram that compares things — graph
10. a lot of money — fortune

Page 53 — Digraphs

A **digraph** is two consonants pronounced as one sound.
Examples: sh as in **sh**ell, ch as in **ch**ew, th as in **th**in

Directions: Write **sh**, **ch**, or **th** to complete each word below.

1. **th**reaten
2. **ch**ill
3. **sh**ock
4. **sh**iver
5. **th**aw
6. **ch**allenge
7. peri**sh**
8. **sh**ield
9. **ch**art
10. **th**rive

Directions: Complete these sentences with a word, or form of the word, from the list above.

1. A trip to the South Pole would really be a (ch) challenge
2. The ice there never (th) thaws because the temperature averages –50°C.
3. How can any living thing (th) thrive or even live when it's so cold?
4. With 6 months of total darkness and those icy temperatures, any plants would soon (sh) perish
5. Even the thought of that numbing cold makes me (sh) shiver
6. The cold and darkness (th) threaten the lives of explorers.
7. The explorers trust take along maps and (ch) charts to help them find their way.
8. Special clothing helps protect and (sh) shield them from the cold.
9. Still, the weather must be a (sh) shock at first.
10. Did someone leave a door open? Suddenly I feel a (ch) chill

Page 54 — Subjects and Verbs

Directions: Underline the subject and verb in each sentence below. Write **S** over the subject and **V** over the verb. If the verb is two words, mark them both.

Examples: Dennis was drinking some punch. The punch was too sweet.

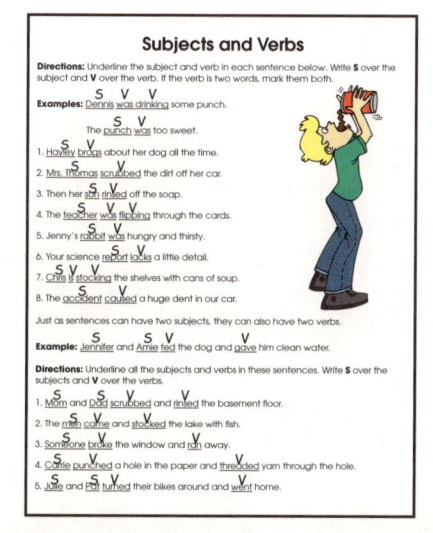

1. Hayley brags about her dog all the time.
2. Mrs. Thomas scrubbed the dirt off her car.
3. Then her son rinsed off the soap.
4. The teacher was flipping through the cards.
5. Jenny's rabbit was hungry and thirsty.
6. Your science report lacks a little detail.
7. Chris is stocking the shelves with cans of soup.
8. The accident caused a huge dent in our car.

Just as sentences can have two subjects, they can also have two verbs.

Example: Jennifer and Amie fed the dog and gave him clean water.

Directions: Underline all the subjects and verbs in these sentences. Write **S** over the subjects and **V** over the verbs.

1. Mom and Dad scrubbed and rinsed the basement floor.
2. The men came and stocked the lake with fish.
3. Someone broke the window and ran away.
4. Carrie punched a hole in the paper and threaded yarn through the hole.
5. Jake and Pat turned their bikes around and went home.

Page 55 — Picture This!

A **compound word** is formed by two or more words. Some compound words are written as one word.
Examples: blueberry, motorcycle
Other compound words are joined by a hyphen.
Examples: twenty-one, editor-in-chief

Directions: Write the compound word for each of the following cartoons.

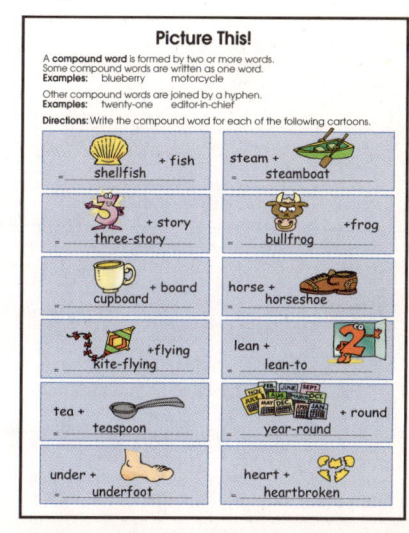

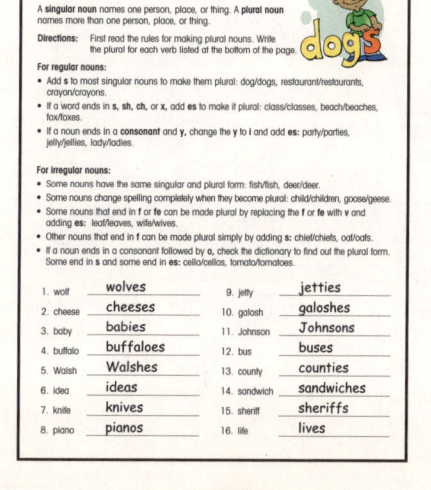

- _ + fish — shellfish
- steam + _ — steamboat
- _ + story — three-story
- _ + frog — bullfrog
- _ + board — cupboard
- horse + _ — horseshoe
- _ + flying — kite-flying
- lean + _ — lean-to
- tea + _ — teaspoon
- _ + round — year-round
- under + _ — underfoot
- heart + _ — heartbroken

Page 56 — Dividing Words

A **syllable** is a unit of sound in a word. Every syllable has only one vowel sound. The following are some rules of syllables.

Use hyphens (-) to divide words.
A one-syllable word is never divided.
When a word has a prefix, divide the word between the prefix and the base word.
Example: repaint → re-paint
When a word has a suffix with a vowel sound in it, divide the word between the base word and the suffix.
Example: cupful → cup-ful

When two or more consonants come between two vowels in a word, the word is usually divided between the first two consonants.
Example: surprise → sur-prise
Divide a compound word between the words that make up the compound word.
Example: airplane → air-plane
When a vowel is sounded alone in a word, it forms a syllable by itself.
Example: monument → mon-u-ment

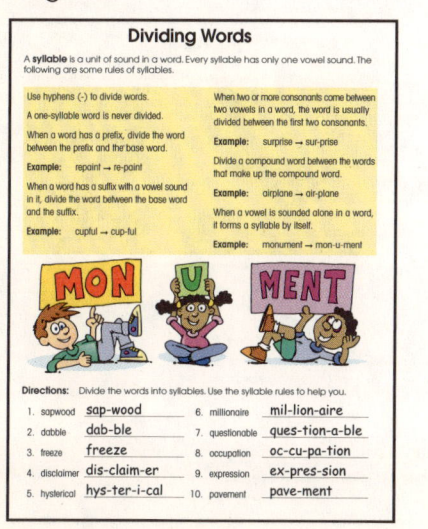

Directions: Divide the words into syllables. Use the syllable rules to help you.

1. sapwood — sap-wood
2. dabble — dab-ble
3. freeze — freeze
4. disclaimer — dis-claim-er
5. hysterical — hys-ter-i-cal
6. millionaire — mil-lion-aire
7. questionable — ques-tion-a-ble
8. occupation — oc-cu-pa-tion
9. expression — ex-pres-sion
10. pavement — pave-ment

Page 57 — Singular or Plural

A **singular noun** names one person, place, or thing. A **plural noun** names more than one person, place, or thing.

Directions: First read the rules for making plural nouns. Write the plural for each word listed at the bottom of the page.

For regular nouns:
- Add **s** to most singular nouns to make them plural: dog/dogs, restaurant/restaurants, crayon/crayons.
- If a noun ends in **s**, **sh**, **ch**, or **x**, add **es** to make it plural: class/classes, beach/beaches, fox/foxes.
- If a noun ends in a **consonant** and **y**, change the **y** to **i** and add **es**: party/parties, jelly/jellies, lady/ladies.

For irregular nouns:
- Some nouns have the same singular and plural form: fish/fish, deer/deer.
- Some nouns change spelling completely when they become plural: child/children, goose/geese.
- Some nouns that end in **f** or **fe** can be made plural by replacing the **f** or **fe** with **v** and adding **es**: leaf/leaves, wife/wives.
- Other nouns that end in **f** can be made plural simply by adding **s**: chief/chiefs, oaf/oafs.
- If a noun ends in a consonant followed by **o**, check the dictionary to find out the plural form. Some end in **s** and some end in **es**: cello/cellos, tomato/tomatoes.

1. wolf — wolves
2. cheese — cheeses
3. baby — babies
4. buffalo — buffaloes
5. Walsh — Walshes
6. idea — ideas
7. knife — knives
8. piano — pianos
9. jetty — jetties
10. galosh — galoshes
11. Johnson — Johnsons
12. bus — buses
13. county — counties
14. sandwich — sandwiches
15. sheriff — sheriffs
16. life — lives

Page 58 — The Plural Surprise

Remember to add **es** to nouns that end in ch, s, sh, ss, x, or z.

Directions: Change each word to a plural by adding **s** or **es**. Write the plural of the word on the space provided.

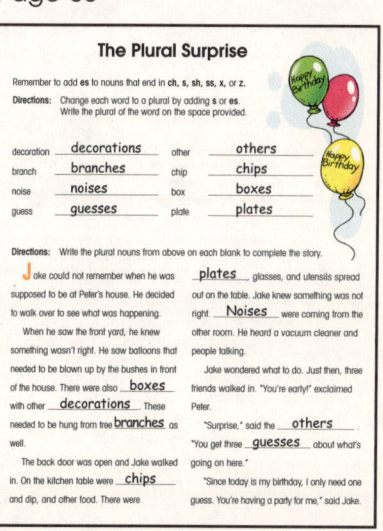

- decoration — decorations
- branch — branches
- noise — noises
- guess — guesses
- other — others
- chip — chips
- box — boxes
- plate — plates

Directions: Write the plural nouns from above on each blank to complete the story.

Jake could not remember when he was supposed to be at Peter's house. He decided to walk over to see what was happening.

When he saw the front yard, he knew something wasn't right. He saw balloons that needed to be blown up by the bushes in front of the house. There were also __boxes__ with other __decorations__. These needed to be hung from tree __branches__ as well.

The back door was open and Jake walked in. On the kitchen table were __chips__ and dip, and other food. There were

__plates__, glasses, and utensils spread out on the table. Jake knew something was not right. __Noises__ were coming from the other room. He heard a vacuum cleaner and people talking.

Jake wondered what to do. Just then, three friends walked in. "You're early!" exclaimed Peter.

"Surprise," said the __others__. "You get three __guesses__ about what's going on here."

"Since today is my birthday, I only need one guess. You're having a party for me," said Jake.

91

Summer Success

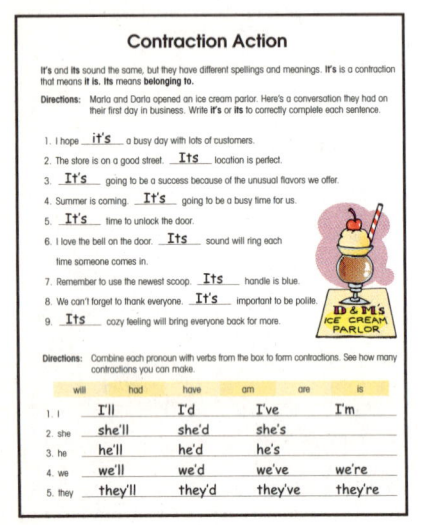

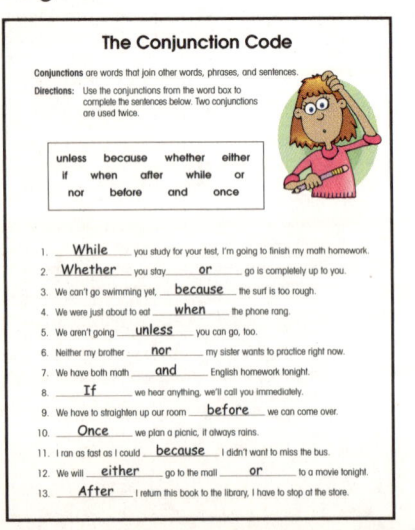

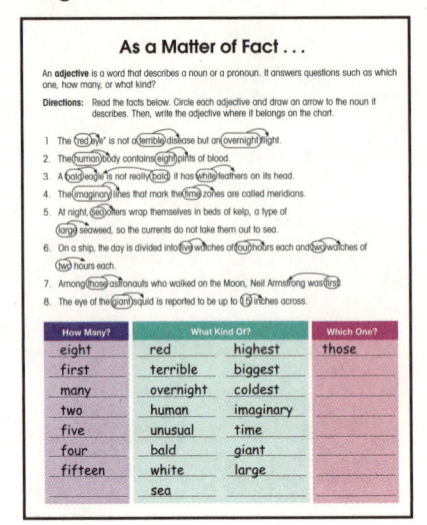

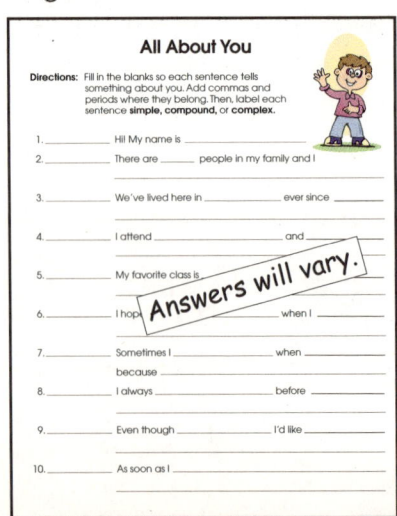

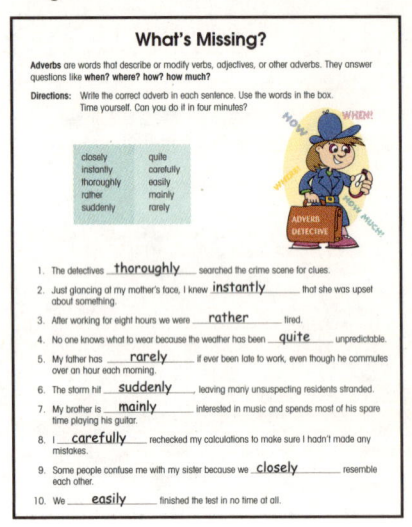

Page 59 — The Art Exhibit

A **verb phrase** consists of one **main verb** and one or more **helping verbs**. The main verb is the most important verb in a verb phrase.

Directions: The following is a list of quotes overheard at Lincoln School's Fall Art Exhibit. Find the verb phrase in each quote. Then, circle the main verb and underline the helping verbs. The first one has been done for you.

1. "Who <u>could have</u> (drawn) that picture?"
2. "Bobby <u>must have been</u> (drawing) since the third grade."
3. "The art department said that they <u>will be</u> (organizing) another exhibit soon."
4. "I <u>am going to</u> (draw) something for the next exhibit."
5. "Eric <u>will</u> (show) his painting, too. He <u>has been</u> (working) on it for the past few weeks."
6. "Any student <u>can be</u> (considered) for one of the exhibits. But only the best work is shown."
7. "We <u>must not</u> (bring) food or drinks to the room; if someone spilled, the artwork <u>could be</u> (ruined)."
8. "That's Mr. Franklin, the art teacher. He <u>will be</u> (showing) off the artwork once everyone is here."
9. "You <u>will</u> (recognize) many of the artists' names."
10. "This is the best exhibit the school <u>has</u> (put on) in two years!"

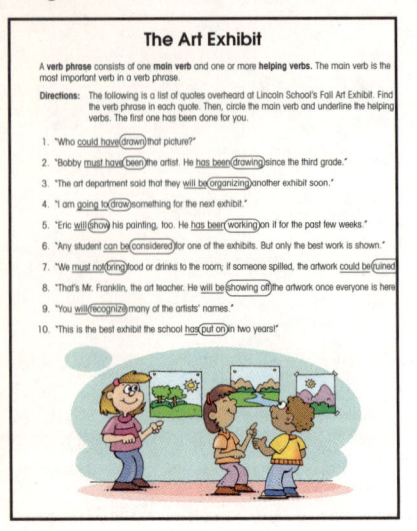

Page 60 — As a Matter of Fact . . .

An **adjective** is a word that describes a noun or a pronoun. It answers questions such as which one, how many, or what kind?

Directions: Read the facts below. Circle each adjective and draw an arrow to the noun it describes. Then, write the adjective where it belongs on the chart.

1. The (red eye) is not a (terrible) disease but an (overnight) flight.
2. The (human) body contains (eight) pints of blood.
3. A (bald) eagle is not really (bald) it has (white) feathers on its head.
4. The (imaginary) lines that mark the (time) zones are called meridians.
5. At night, (sea) otters wrap themselves in beds of kelp, a type of (large) seaweed, so the currents do not take them out to sea.
6. On a ship, the day is divided into (two) watches of (four) hours each and (two) watches of (two) hours each.
7. Among (those) astronauts who walked on the Moon, Neil Armstrong was (first).
8. The eye of the (giant) squid is reported to be up to (15) inches across.

How Many?	What Kind Of?	Which One?
eight	red	those
first	terrible	biggest
many	overnight	coldest
two	human	imaginary
five	unusual	time
four	bald	giant
fifteen	white	large
	sea	

Page 61 — What's Missing?

Adverbs are words that describe or modify verbs, adjectives, or other adverbs. They answer questions like **when? where? how? how much?**

Directions: Write the correct adverb in each sentence. Use the words in the box. Time yourself. Can you do it in four minutes?

closely	quite
instantly	carefully
thoroughly	easily
rather	mainly
suddenly	rarely

1. The detectives __thoroughly__ searched the crime scene for clues.
2. Just glancing at my mother's face, I knew __instantly__ that she was upset about something.
3. After working for eight hours we were __rather__ tired.
4. No one knows what to wear because the weather has been __quite__ unpredictable.
5. My father has __rarely__ if ever been late to work, even though he commutes over an hour each morning.
6. The storm hit __suddenly__ leaving many unsuspecting residents stranded.
7. My brother is __mainly__ interested in music and spends most of his spare time playing his guitar.
8. I __carefully__ rechecked my calculations to make sure I hadn't made any mistakes.
9. Some people confuse me with my sister because we __closely__ resemble each other.
10. We __easily__ finished the test in no time at all.

Page 62 — Contraction Action

It's and **its** sound the same, but they have different spellings and meanings. **It's** is a contraction that means **it is**. **Its** means **belonging to**.

Directions: Marla and Darla opened an ice cream parlor. Here's a conversation they had on their first day in business. Write **it's** or **its** to correctly complete each sentence.

1. I hope __it's__ a busy day with lots of customers.
2. The store is on a good street. __Its__ location is perfect.
3. __It's__ going to be a success because of the unusual flavors we offer.
4. Summer is coming. __It's__ going to be a busy time for us.
5. __It's__ time to unlock the door.
6. I love the bell on the door. __Its__ sound will ring each time someone comes in.
7. Remember to use the newest scoop. __Its__ handle is blue.
8. We can't forget to thank everyone. __It's__ important to be polite.
9. __Its__ cozy feeling will bring everyone back for more.

Directions: Combine each pronoun with verbs from the box to form contractions. See how many contractions you can make.

	will	had	have	am	are	is
1. I	I'll	I'd	I've	I'm		
2. she	she'll	she'd				she's
3. he	he'll	he'd				he's
4. we	we'll	we'd	we've		we're	
5. they	they'll	they'd	they've		they're	

Page 63 — The Babysitter's List

The, an and **a** are called **articles**. Articles are a special kind of adjective. **The** is always used to refer to a specific noun, so it is called a **definite article**. **A** and **an** refer to any noun, so they are called **indefinite articles**.

Directions: Help Mrs. Farkle complete the list of instructions she made for the babysitter. Write the correct article on the line in each sentence.

1. We'll be at __the__ Golden Dragon Restaurant until 8:00.
   We are going to __the__ movies after dinner.
2. You can make __a__ simple dinner.
3. There is pizza in __the__ freezer.
   There is also fruit in __a__ bowl on the table.
4. Have __the__ kids use paper plates.
   Otherwise, they'll make __a__ huge mess!
5. For dessert each child can have __an__ apple.
6. There are emergency phone numbers near __the__ kitchen phone.
7. The kids can watch __a__ video if they want.
8. Read __a__ book to __the__ kids at bedtime.
9. Please do not talk on __the__ phone for longer than five minutes.
10. If you watch TV after the kids go to bed, keep __the__ volume low.
11. You can have __a__ snack whenever you want!

Page 64 — Is That a Fact?

A **preposition** is a word that shows how one word is related to another in a sentence. A **prepositional phrase** is a group of words that begins with a preposition and ends with a noun or pronoun.

Directions: Each fact below is missing a prepositional phrase. Use the code to figure out each one. Write the phrase on each line.

A B C D E F G H I J K L M
N O P Q R S T U V W X Y Z

1. The Iditarod is a 1,200-mile dogsled race __over ice and snow__.
2. Air rushes __through your nose__ at 100 miles per hour when you sneeze.
3. Red is the most commonly found color __in national flags__.
4. The Islands of Hawaii evolved as volcanoes erupted __under the Pacific Ocean__.
5. French fries are not really __from France__ but __from Belguim__.
6. Bertrand Piccard and Brian Jones were the first to fly __around the world__ nonstop __in a balloon__.

Page 65 — The Conjunction Code

Conjunctions are words that join other words, phrases, and sentences.

Directions: Use the conjunctions from the word box to complete the sentences below. Two conjunctions are used twice.

unless	because	whether	either
if	when	after	while	or
nor	before	and	once	

1. __While__ you study for your test, I'm going to finish my math homework.
2. __Whether__ you stay __or__ go is completely up to you.
3. We can't go swimming yet, __because__ the surf is too rough.
4. We were just about to eat __when__ the phone rang.
5. We aren't going __unless__ you can go, too.
6. Neither my brother __nor__ my sister wants to practice right now.
7. We have both math __and__ English homework tonight.
8. __If__ we hear anything, we'll call you immediately.
9. We have to straighten up our room __before__ we can come over.
10. __Once__ we plan a picnic, it always rains.
11. I ran as fast as I could __because__ I didn't want to miss the bus.
12. We will __either__ go to the mall __or__ to a movie tonight.
13. __After__ I return this book to the library, I have to stop at the store.

Page 66 — All About You

Directions: Fill in the blanks so each sentence tells something about you. Add commas and periods where they belong. Then, label each sentence **simple**, **compound**, or **complex**.

1. _____ Hi! My name is _____
2. _____ There are _____ people in my family and I
3. _____ We've lived here in _____ ever since _____
4. _____ I attend _____ and _____
5. _____ My favorite class is _____
6. _____ I hope _____ when I
7. _____ Sometimes I _____ when _____ because
8. _____ I always _____ before _____
9. _____ Even though _____ I'd like
10. _____ As soon as I

Answers will vary.

Page 67 — The List

Underline titles of books, magazines, works of art, plays, movies, television shows, and names of ships and planes. Use quotation marks around titles of chapters, short stories, short poems, and songs.

Directions: Here's Miss Muffet's list of the Top Ten Things to Do While on Vacation. The little Miss's list has a few errors, though. Help her out by underlining and adding quotation marks to titles and names as necessary.

1. Practice my dramatic reading of "The Spider and the Fly" for my appearance on <u>Star Search</u>.
2. Rent the movie of E.B. White's <u>Charlotte's Web</u>.
3. Record my rock version of "Eensy Weensy Spider" and send to the Backstreet Boys.
4. Finish my article, "How to Live With Spiders and Like It," for <u>Ranger Rick</u>.
5. Go for a ride on the <u>Out to Sea</u>, my friend Bobby Shafto's private yacht.
6. Read the chapter "Major Order of Arachnids" in <u>Kids' Guide to Insects & Spiders</u>.
7. Get tickets for <u>Tarantella</u>, the new Broadway musical that everyone's talking about.
8. Arrange for a screen test for a possible role in the sequel to <u>Arachnophobia</u>.

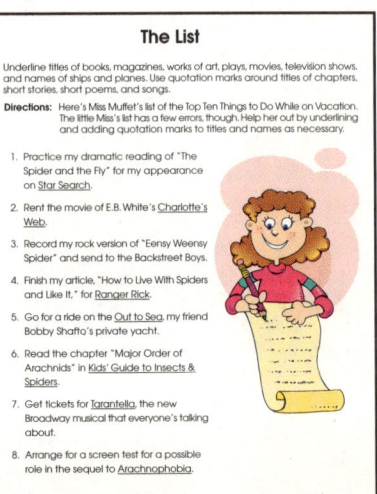

92

Summer Success

Page 68

Game Show Contestants

Sometimes you need to **infer,** or make an educated guess, about information that is missing from a selection. Use details from the selection and your own experience to make inferences.

Directions: Read the story. Then use story details to infer the identity of each contestant. Write each contestant's name on the line below the correct picture.

Jill — Gary — Nellie

Lena — Sam — Vinnie

The two teams were preparing for the game show to start. On the first team, Nellie was busy reciting math formulas backwards and forwards. Jill was doing push-ups at the front of the stage to calm her nerves. Vinnie chimed in, "Hey, are you doing push-ups? This is a game to test how smart you are, not how strong… but then, what do you care, you already have the smartest kid in school on your team! Did I tell you about the time my sister was on a game show? She…."

Vinnie kept talking but no one was really listening. Gary had his hands full putting plastic spiders under Sam's chair, hoping he might distract Sam when it was his turn to answer a question. Sam didn't know about the spiders, but he looked like he was about to cry anyway; he hated having to sit on the stage and speak in front of a group of people. He was especially worried because his team was still missing a contestant, Lena, who was always late.

Finally, Lena arrived and Vinnie started to complain. "Lena, how is our team supposed to win if you can't even show up on time? I was just saying to my best friend the other day that . . ."

Lena interrupted him. "Stick a sock in it, Vinnie, or I'll steal your lunch money like I did last week."

Page 69

Why Write?

There are four main purposes for writing: to **inform**, to **entertain,** to **persuade,** and to **express** feelings, opinions, or beliefs.

Directions: Think about the writing that you have read. Then, decide whether each of the following statements is true or false. Follow the directions.

1. Writers can only write for one purpose at a time.
   If true, circle the letter in box # 16.
   If false, circle the letter in box # 18.
2. Informative writing is always the most fun to read.
   If true, circle the letter in box # 14.
   If false, circle the letter in box # 4.
3. Writers who write to inform their readers don't ever try to write to entertain.
   If true, circle the letter in box # 25.
   If false, circle the letter in box # 12.
4. Writers who write to inform include many facts in their work.
   If true, circle the letter in box # 20.
   If false, circle the letter in box # 3.
5. Writers who write to inform should never express opinions in their work.
   If true, circle the letter in box # 8.
   If false, circle the letter in box # 1.
6. Good persuasive writers also provide information on their topics.
   If true, circle the letter in box # 7.
   If false, circle the letter in box # 21.
7. It is easier to write to entertain people than it is to write to inform them.
   If true, circle the letter in box # 15.
   If false, circle the letter in box # 11.
8. When writers write to inform their readers, they can also entertain them with interesting facts and stories.
   If true, circle the letter in box # 22.
   If false, circle the letter in box # 5.
9. A story about a struggle with illness is a good example of writing with a main purpose of expressing feelings, opinions, or beliefs.
   If true, circle the letter in box # 10. If false, circle the letter in box # 29.

(E)	A	T	(X)	N
H	(C)	S	M	(E)
(L)	(L)	R	A	I
V	B	(E)	D	(N)
U	(T)	R	O	G

Now, write all the circled letters, in order, to complete this sentence:

If you set your mind to it, you can be an E X C E L L E N T writer!

Page 70

What's the Main Idea?

Often the main idea of a passage is **stated** in a sentence. Sometimes, however, you have to figure out the **unstated** main idea by looking at important details.

Directions: Read each paragraph. Then, write a sentence that states the main idea for each paragraph.

One of the most popular forms of entertainment today is playing computer games. Children are fascinated by these games. They are popular because they have exciting graphics, fun activities, and a wide variety of games.

Stated Main Idea: One of the most popular forms of entertainment today is playing computer games.

Some radio stations play jazz. Others play rock. Still others play country. Some stations just report the news and weather. What a lot of variety we get from radio!

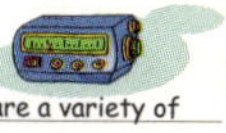

Unstated Main Idea: Possible answer: There are a variety of listening options on the radio.

Do you have a hobby? One kind of hobby involves collecting things. Some people collect stamps. Others may collect dolls or stuffed animals. Many people collect and trade sports cards. Another kind of hobby involves building things. Some people build models of ships and airplanes from kits or build large structures from Legos. Other hobbies involve music, art, dance, and sports.

Unstated Main Idea: Possible answer: There are many kinds of hobbies.

Page 71

Compare! Contrast! Choose!

Directions: Kobe wants to buy a bike and has saved $125. He found some information about one bike from a company online. He also cut out an ad from the newspaper for a similar bike. Help Kobe compare and contrast the two bikes. Complete the chart.

Rally Boy's Mountain Master

When it comes to bicycles for active, hard-playing boys, ages 10-14, sturdiness and safety are essential. This yellow and black 24" wheel Mountain Master offers both and is sure to please both parents and kids. It features a unique oversized frame that makes getting on and off a snap, a large derailleur guard, alloy hubs and rims, and many other dependable components. A 21-speed drive train makes riding effortless. The twist shifters come equipped with an easy-to-read gear display to let you know what gear you're in. Top-notch linear pull brakes allow young riders to stop when they need to. The 1.95-inch all-terrain tires perform well on any surface. Your cost is only $229.99.*

*Price does not include shipping. Delivery 4-5 working days. Assembly required.

FOR SALE
Used boy's 24" blue Rally Mountain King bike
21-speed, easy-to-read gear shift display, pull brakes, large derailleur guard and an extra set of 1.95 all-terrain tires. Just a year old, still like new. Perfect for a 10- to 14-year-old boy. Come and check it out. Take it for a spin around the block. Asking only $100. Call 555-1234 for more details.

Compare

Rally bikes	same size
Similar features	for riders 10-14

Contrast

black and yellow	blue
$229.99 + shipping	$100
new	used
assembly required	ready to ride
can't test ride	can test ride
no extra tires	extra set of tires

If you were Kobe, which bike would you buy? Why?
Answers will vary.

Page 72

What a Character!

Directions: Who is your favorite TV character? List words to describe the character on the left side of the Venn diagram. Do the same for your favorite character from a book, listing his or her traits on the right. Make sure that any traits the two share are listed in the middle. Then, answer the questions at the bottom of the page.

Favorite TV Character: ____________ Favorite Book Character: ____________

Show: ____________ Book title: ____________

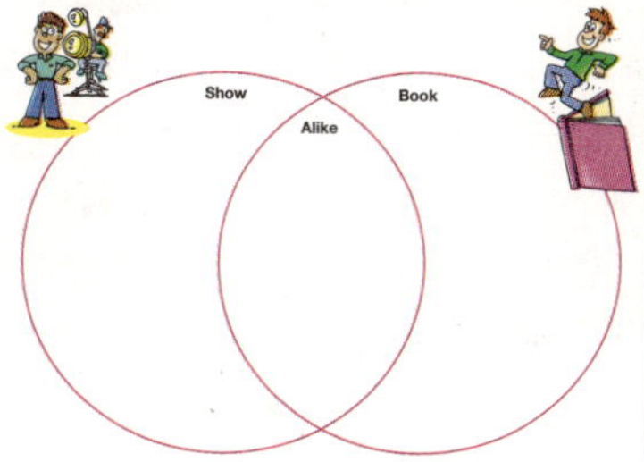

1. What is your favorite TV character's most unusual trait? ____________
2. What is your favorite book character's most unusual trait? ____________

Page 73

Plot Out the Action

The **plot** is the main storyline in any work of fiction. The most important parts of a plot are:

background: the introduction; what the reader needs to know about the characters and the general situation	**conflict:** the problem that the main character/characters must solve or the goal that he/she/they want to achieve	**rising action:** what the characters do to overcome the conflict; this may include encountering more problems	**climax:** usually the most exciting part of the story, often when character(s) must resolve the conflict	**falling action:** events that occur after the conflict has been resolved

Directions: Read this story about Luis. Then, answer the questions at the bottom of the page. Make sure to use complete sentences.

Luis' mom needed his help. She was planning a backyard party for his grandmother. She was so busy getting the house ready, she needed someone to help her do the shopping. She gave Luis her shopping list and $40.

Luis had been to the store many times before but never by himself. He got a cart and walked up the first aisle. As he put each item in the cart, he crossed it off the list.

While he was in the snacks aisle, he decided to add some things to the cart. His mom had only written pretzels on the list, but he put potato chips and popcorn in the cart, too. In the drink section, Luis added orange drinks and root beer.

When he got to the checkout, the cashier told him that the total was $47.25. But Luis only had $40. He couldn't believe his mother hadn't given him enough money! Then, he remembered that he had put extra things in the cart. He asked the cashier if he could put some of his items back. When she told him yes, he gave back the extra snacks and drinks. By doing this, he brought the total down to $38.

When Luis arrived home with the groceries, he unpacked them and told his mom what had happened. She thanked him and told him that next time he went to the grocery store, she would give him some extra money. That way he could choose something special to buy as a reward for helping her out!

1. Give the background for this story. Luis' mom is too busy to go to the store.
2. What is the main conflict in this story? Luis must go to the store by himself for the first time.
3. Describe the rising action of the story. Luis decides on a plan when in the store. He picks up more food than is on his list. He doesn't have enough money to pay for all the items in his cart. He puts the extra food back so he can pay for the items on his mother's list.

Page 74

So Much Fiction!

Directions: Read about the different types of fiction. Then, label each book description below with the correct type of fiction.

Realistic fiction has characters and events like those in real life. It is set in a place that is or seems real.

Fantasy is about impossible events and is often set in an unreal world.

Science fiction is fantasy based on science. It often takes place in the future and sometimes in outer space.

A **mystery** may seem realistic. Its plot is based on a puzzle that the main characters (and reader) try to solve.

A **fable** is a short story that teaches a lesson. Its characters are often animals.

A **folktale** was first told aloud and was handed down from generation to generation. It may explain how some feature of nature came to exist.

1. science fiction
Have Space Suit, Will Travel
by Robert Heinlein
Kip Russell is in the backyard of his house when he is kidnapped by the Mother Thing and taken to the moon. He travels to Luna and the Magellenic cloud—and learns he must help save the Earth.

2. folk tale
The Story of the Milky Way: A Cherokee Tale
by Joseph Bruchac, illustrated by Virginia A. Stroud
Villagers cleverly frighten away a thieving spirit dog. As it leaps into the sky, grains of stolen cornmeal fall from its mouth and become stars.

3. mystery
Mandie and the Secret Tunnel
by Lois Gladys Leppard
It is the year 1900, and Mandie is searching her dead uncle's mansion for a missing will when she finds a secret tunnel and strangers who claim to be relatives. But can they help her with her search?

4. realistic fiction
Beezus and Ramona
by Beverly Cleary
Beezus wishes she could love her little sister, Ramona. But Ramona keeps doing things to make Beezus just furious!

5. fable
The Little Red Ant and the Great Big Crumb
by Shirley Climo, illustrated by Francisco X. Mora
A small red ant finds a delicious crumb in a Mexican cornfield. She asks many animals to help her move it, but finally she learns a lesson about who is the strongest of all.

6. fantasy
Harry Potter and the Prisoner of Azkaban
by J.K. Rowling
It is vacation and Harry runs away from his uncle's house because he has accidentally caused horrible Aunt Marge to turn into a drifting balloon. He thinks he's safe when a purple bus carries him off, but his dangerous adventures have just begun.

Page 75

Sort and Shelve

Directions: Read about the different types of nonfiction. Then, look at the books shown below. On the line underneath each book, write the type of nonfiction it is.

An **informational book** gives facts about a topic and may contain the writer's opinions.

A **how-to book** gives directions for an activity.

A **reference book** presents a specialized type of information in a very organized way.

A **textbook** presents facts in one subject area and often gives a broad general view of the subject. It does not contain opinions.

A **biography** is the true story of someone's life, written by someone else.

An **autobiography** is the true story of the writer's life up to that time.

A **personal narrative** focuses on an important event in the writer's life.

personal narrative — biography — autobiography — reference book

informational book — textbook — how-to book

Page 76

The Missing Painting

Directions: Read the following mystery and answer the questions.

Detective Doolittle couldn't sleep. He … "And you didn't see or hear anything strange …

1. He knows that she is lying because she said she saw Fred at the Post Office the day after the robbery, which must have been a Sunday, but the Post Office isn't open on Sundays. Also, she said that the gardener had to take her daughter to school that day, but there is definitely no school on a Saturday in July.

2. Answers will vary, but may include: Miss Rappaport probably made up the whole story about the painting being stolen. There's no evidence and she's trying to blame it on everyone else.

1. Why does Detective Doolittle say that Miss Rappaport is lying?
2. What do you think happened to the painting? What makes you think so?
3. On another sheet of paper, write a conclusion to the story.

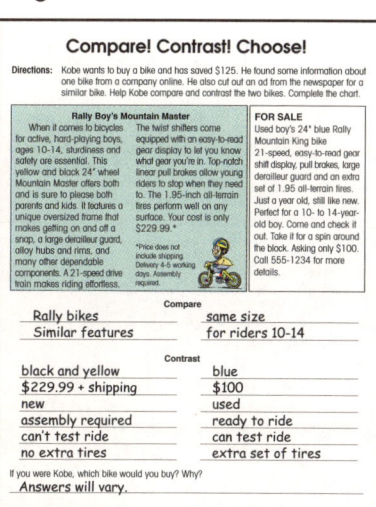

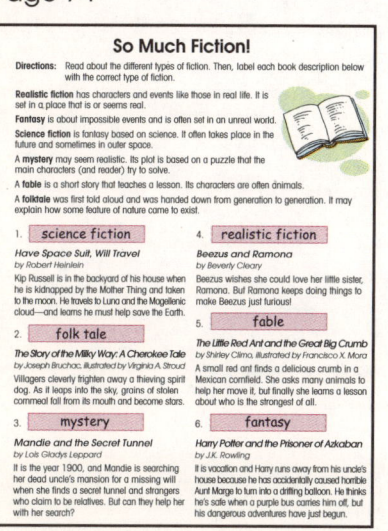

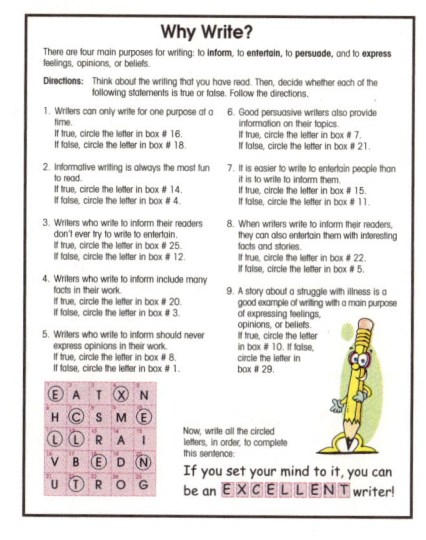

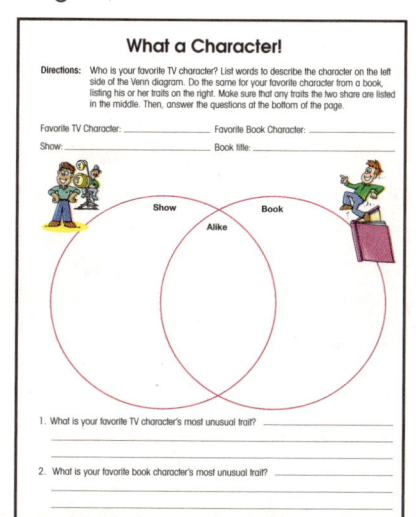

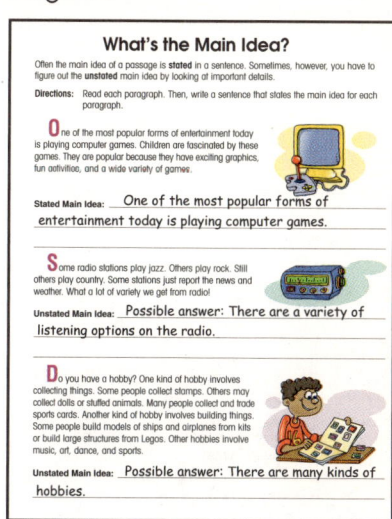

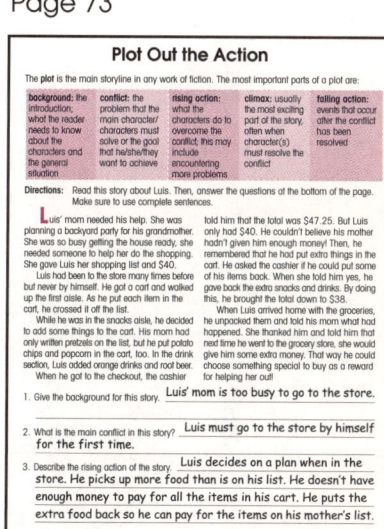

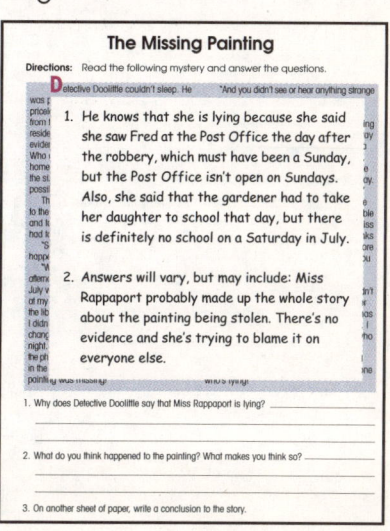

Summer Success

Page 77

Fact or Opinion?

What is the difference between a fact and an opinion? **Facts** can be proven true. **Opinions** are beliefs, judgments, or feelings that cannot be verified.

Directions: Each of the following sentences contains a fact and an opinion. Underline the part that states a fact, and put brackets around each part that states an opinion.

1. [The most exciting place to tour in Washington, D.C. is the White House,] which has been the home and office of every U.S. President except George Washington.
2. The capital was named after George Washington, our nation's first President [and the greatest general in our nation's history.]
3. The Washington Monument is a 555-foot white marble obelisk [that is enjoyed by every visitor to our nation's capital.]
4. [I think the Declaration of Independence, the Constitution, and the Bill of Rights are our nation's most important historic documents,] and they are on display at the National Archives.
5. The National Air and Space Museum is one of the Smithsonian Institution's 14 museums [and the most interesting one of all.]
6. The National Zoo is also part of the Smithsonian, [and it's a terrific place for families to visit.]
7. [The Lincoln Memorial is a beautiful monument,] and it includes a gigantic statue of Abraham Lincoln, our 16th President.
8. The dome of the Capitol is visible from many parts of the city [and is a spectacular sight.]
9. There is an exhibit for children over eight years old at the U.S. Holocaust Memorial Museum called Daniel's Story, [but I think everyone should see it.]
10. The National Gallery of Art, located on the Mall, [is without a doubt the world's greatest art museum.]

Page 78

Report-a-Sauras, Part 1

Directions: You are writing a report about dinosaurs. In each paragraph, you want to answer a certain research question. The following is a list of notes you took at the library. Write each piece of information under the paragraph it goes with.

- Dinosaurs roamed the earth for more than 180 million years, but they became extinct over 65 million years ago.
- By studying fossils, paleontologists can learn about the sizes of the different dinosaurs.
- Almost everything we know about dinosaurs comes from looking at fossils.
- Scientists who study dinosaur fossils are called paleontologists.
- Before paleontologists can study fossils, they must dig them from the ground and clean them very carefully.
- Then, the fossils can be taken to a university or museum and studied.
- By studying fossils, paleontologists can learn what the different types of dinosaurs ate.
- Fossils were formed from dinosaurs when their remains hardened into stone or were surrounded by mud or sand that hardened into stone.
- Fossils are formed over long periods of time from the bones, eggs, and other remains of dinosaurs.
- By studying fossils, paleontologists can learn how the different types of dinosaurs cared for their young.

First paragraph: When did the dinosaurs live?
· Dinosaurs roamed the earth for more than 180 million years, but they became extinct over 65 million years ago.

Second paragraph: What are fossils, and why are they important?
· Almost everything we know about dinosaurs comes from looking at fossils.
· Fossils were formed from dinosaurs when these remains hardened into stone or were surrounded by mud or sand that hardened into stone.
· Fossils are formed over long periods of time from the bones, eggs, and other remains of dinosaurs.

Page 79

Report-a-Sauras, Part 2

Directions: Continue to write each piece of information from page 78 under the paragraph it goes with.

Third paragraph: What are paleontologists, and what do they do?
· Scientists who study dinosaur fossils are called paleontologists.
· Before paleontologists can study fossils, they must dig them from the ground and clean them very carefully.
· Then the fossils can be taken to a university or museum and studied.

Fourth paragraph: What can paleontologists learn from looking at fossils?
· By studying fossils, paleontologists can learn about the sizes of the different dinosaurs.
· By studying fossils, paleontologists can learn what the different types of dinosaurs ate.
· By studying fossils, paleontologists can learn how the different types of dinosaurs cared for their young.

Page 80

Proofreading Puzzler

Directions: Proofread the following article for capitalization, punctuation, grammar, and spelling mistakes. Use the proofreading symbols below to mark any mistakes you find.

ℐ delete	# space	⌿ lowercase
∧ insert	≡ capitalize	¶ new paragraph
⁀ transpose		

What do a Saint Bernard, a Chihuahua, and a german Shepherd have in common? That's easy—they are all dogs! But why don't all dogs look alike? Most terriers are small and low to the ground. Long ago, terriers were used to hunt rats and badgers. The dogs would follow the rats and badgers into their underground homes. Terriers are good diggers; their small size helps them get into tight places.

Greyhounds are racing dogs. They run very fast. a greyhound's long legs help it run. Another part of this dog's body that helps it run is its lungs. Just look at the greyhound's large chest! This dog's lungs are large and can hold a lot of air.

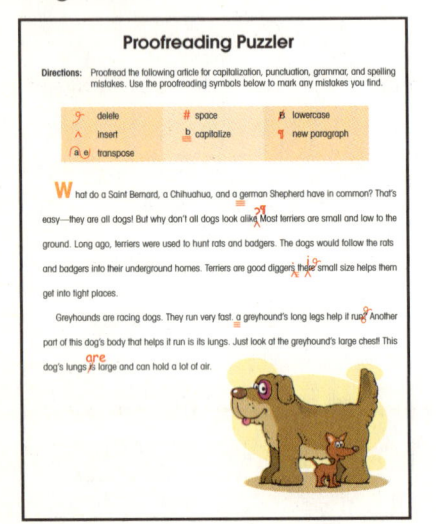

Page 81

Similes Are Like Metaphors

Using **similes** and **metaphors** makes writing interesting. They are ways of describing things.

Similes are comparisons that use **like** or **as**.

Examples: She looked like a frightened mouse.
She looked as frightened as a mouse.

Metaphors are direct comparisons that **do not use like** or **as**.

Example: She was a frightened mouse.

Directions: Rewrite each sentence two different ways to make it more interesting. In the first sentence (a), add at least one adjective and one adverb. In the second sentence (b), compare something in the sentence to something else, using a simile or metaphor.

Example: The baby cried.
a. The sick baby cried softly all night.
b. The baby cried louder and louder, like a storm gaining strength.

1. The stranger arrived.
   a.
   b.
2. The dog barked.
   a.
   b.
3. The children danced.
   a.
   b.
4. The moon rose.
   a.
   b.

Sentences will vary.

Page 82

Using a Dictionary

Directions: Use the dictionary entry below to answer the questions.

ad-he-sive (ad-he′-siv) *adj.* 1. Tending to adhere; sticky. 2. Gummed so as to adhere. *n.* 3. An adhesive substance such as paste or glue. **ad-he-sive-ly** *adv.* **ad-he-sive-ness** *n.*

1. Based on the first definition of **adhesive**, what do you think **adhere** means? **to stick to something**
2. Which definition of **adhesive** is used in this sentence? The tape was so adhesive that we couldn't peel it loose. **tending to adhere, sticky**
3. Which part of speech is **adhesive** used as in this sentence? We put a strong adhesive on the package to keep is sealed. **noun**
4. How many syllables does **adhesive** have? **three**
5. Is **adhesive** used as a noun or an adjective in this sentence? The adhesive we chose to use was not very gummy. **noun**
6. **Adhesive** and variations of the word can be used as what parts of speech? **noun, adjective, adverb**

Directions: Write sentences using these words.

7. adhesiveness
8. adhesively
9. adhere

Answers will vary.

Page 83

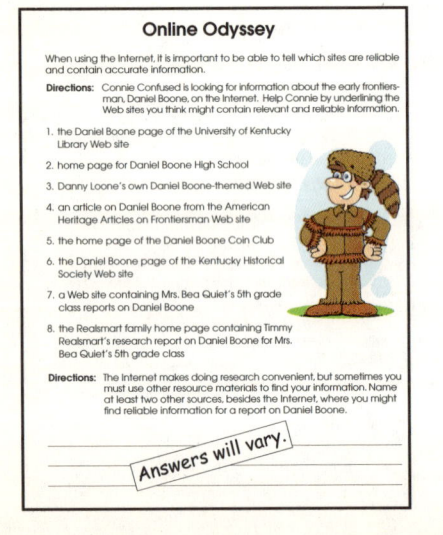

Online Odyssey

When using the Internet, it is important to be able to tell which sites are reliable and contain accurate information.

Directions: Connie Confused is looking for information about the early frontiersman, Daniel Boone, on the Internet. Help Connie by underlining the Web sites you think might contain relevant and reliable information.

1. the Daniel Boone page of the University of Kentucky Library Web site
2. home page for Daniel Boone High School
3. Danny Loone's own Daniel Boone-themed Web site
4. an article on Daniel Boone from the American Heritage Articles on Frontiersman Web site
5. the home page of the Daniel Boone Coin Club
6. the Daniel Boone page of the Kentucky Historical Society Web site
7. a Web site containing Mrs. Bea Quiet's 5th grade class reports on Daniel Boone
8. the Realsmart family home page containing Timmy Realsmart's research report on Daniel Boone for Mrs. Bea Quiet's 5th grade class

Directions: The Internet makes doing research convenient, but sometimes you must use other resource materials to find your information. Name at least two other sources, besides the Internet, where you might find reliable information for a report on Daniel Boone.

Answers will vary.

94

Curriculum Skills for Fourth-Grade Success

McGraw-Hill, the premier education publisher PreK–12, wants to be your partner in helping you educate your child. **Summer Success** was designed to help your child retain those skills learned during the past school year. With **Summer Success,** your child will be ready to review and master new material with confidence when he or she returns to school in the fall.

Use this checklist—compiled from state curriculum standards—to help your child prepare for proficiency testing. Place a check mark in the box if the appropriate skill has been mastered. If your child needs more work with a particular skill, place an "R" in the box and come back to it for review.

Math Skills

- ❏ Understands place value through 999,999.
- ❏ Uses problem-solving strategies—such as rounding, regrouping, using multiple operations, and Venn diagrams—to solve numerical and word problems.
- ❏ Compares whole numbers using < > =.
- ❏ Solves multiple-operation problems using a calculator.
- ❏ Adds and subtracts proper fractions having like denominators of 12 or less.
- ❏ Adds and subtracts simple decimals in context of money with and without regrouping.
- ❏ Tells and writes time shown on traditional and digital clocks.
- ❏ Uses customary system to measure length, mass, volume, and temperature.
- ❏ Uses metric system to measure length, mass, volume, and temperature.
- ❏ Selects the appropriate operational and relational symbols to make an expression true ($4 \times 3=12$).
- ❏ Recognizes and uses commutative and associative properties of multiplication ($5 \times 7=35$...What is 7×5?).
- ❏ Measures length, width, perimeter, and area to solve numerical and word problems.
- ❏ Describes, draws, identifies, and analyzes two- and three-dimensional shapes.
- ❏ Identifies congruent shapes.
- ❏ Identifies lines of symmetry in shapes.
- ❏ Recognizes patterns and relationships using a bar graph and locating points on a grid.
- ❏ Analyzes and solves simple probability problems.
- ❏ Adds and subtracts with two and three digits, regrouping when necessary.
- ❏ Multiplies two-digit numbers with regrouping, and divides one and two-digit numbers by divisors of 6 – 10, with and without remainders.

Skills

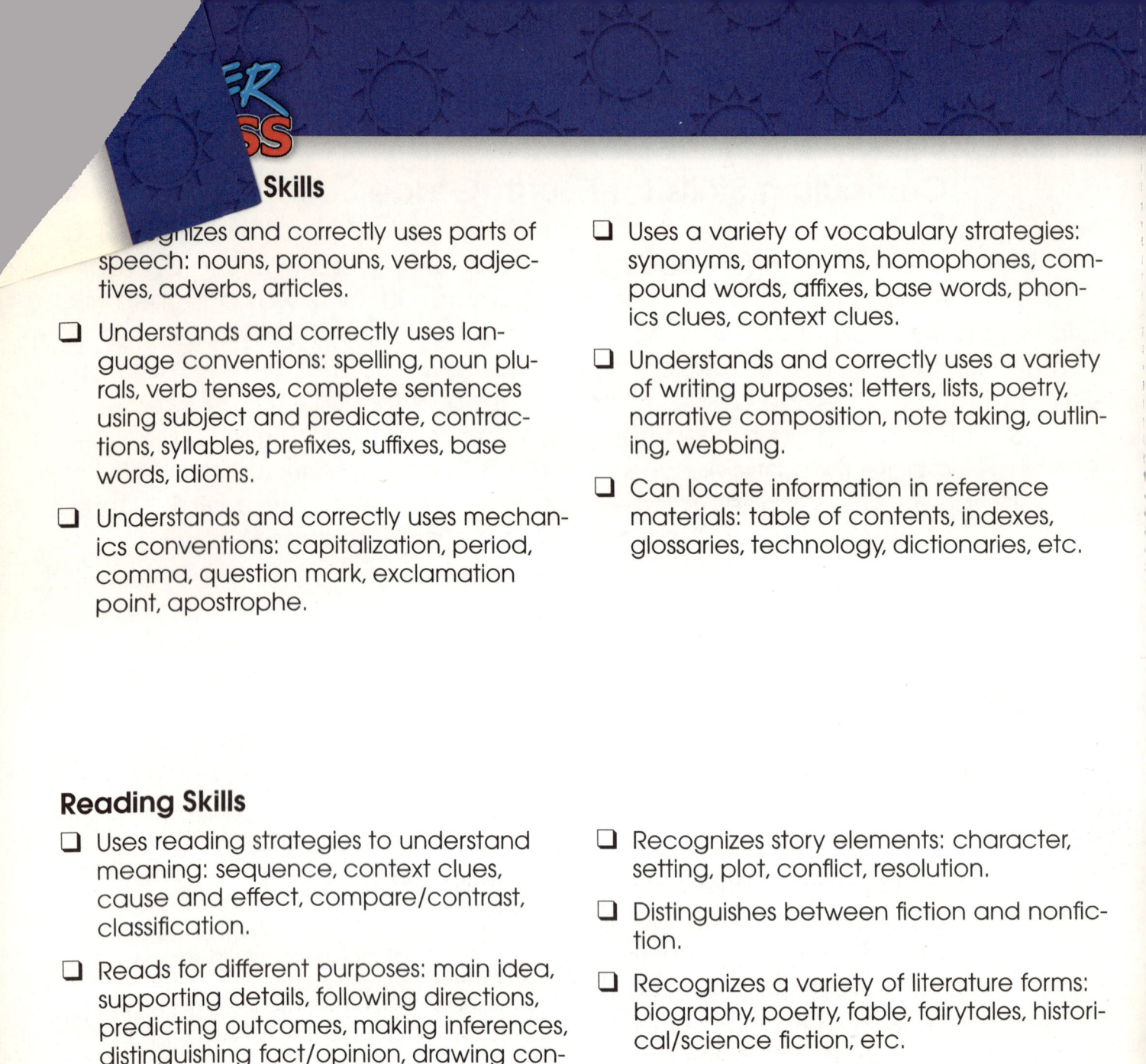

- ☐ Recognizes and correctly uses parts of speech: nouns, pronouns, verbs, adjectives, adverbs, articles.
- ☐ Understands and correctly uses language conventions: spelling, noun plurals, verb tenses, complete sentences using subject and predicate, contractions, syllables, prefixes, suffixes, base words, idioms.
- ☐ Understands and correctly uses mechanics conventions: capitalization, period, comma, question mark, exclamation point, apostrophe.
- ☐ Uses a variety of vocabulary strategies: synonyms, antonyms, homophones, compound words, affixes, base words, phonics clues, context clues.
- ☐ Understands and correctly uses a variety of writing purposes: letters, lists, poetry, narrative composition, note taking, outlining, webbing.
- ☐ Can locate information in reference materials: table of contents, indexes, glossaries, technology, dictionaries, etc.

Reading Skills

- ☐ Uses reading strategies to understand meaning: sequence, context clues, cause and effect, compare/contrast, classification.
- ☐ Reads for different purposes: main idea, supporting details, following directions, predicting outcomes, making inferences, distinguishing fact/opinion, drawing conclusions.
- ☐ Recognizes story elements: character, setting, plot, conflict, resolution.
- ☐ Distinguishes between fiction and nonfiction.
- ☐ Recognizes a variety of literature forms: biography, poetry, fable, fairytales, historical/science fiction, etc.